Comfy Christian

Christopher Scott Nooe

Comfy Christian

Moving from a Spiritual Couch Potato to a Warrior for God

VMI Publishers • Sisters, Oregon

Unless otherwise indicated, Bible quotations are taken from the *Holy Bible: New International Version*. Copyright 1973, 1978, 1984 by International Bible Society.

Published by
VMI Publishers
Sisters, Oregon
www.vmipublishers.com

ISBN: 1933204613
ISBN 13: 9781933204611
Library of Congress Control Number: 2008927917
Printed in the USA.

Dedication

To my father and mother, Dan and Nola,
two crazy kids who had the courage and compassion to
love a small boy unconditionally.

And to my wife, Angela, a truly captivating lady
who has blessed me more than words can say.

CONTENTS

ACKNOWLEDGMENTS

Many Thanks…

— To my parents for your love, support, friendship and sacrifice
— To my wife for being my beauty, my bride, my comforter, supporter and
  completer
— To my kids Gianna, Isaac, Luke and Isabella for keeping me young while
  wearing me out.
— To my brother Phil for jumping in the front seat of the roller coaster
  with me.
— To my friends and family for your heartfelt thoughts and prayers—I
  needed every one of them!
— To the gang at the *Java House* for giving me a caffeine-rich home away
  from home.

PART 1

The Comfy Life

Chapter One

Little Man

*"Before I formed you in the womb I knew you, before
you were born I set you apart."*

JEREMIAH 1:5

I pulled into town at 2:00 A.M. I had driven from Detroit after my daughter's kindergarten orientation. I was not going to miss that. As I checked into the hotel, I knew I would have about two hours to sleep before meeting up with co-workers and enduring another day in the car visiting customers. All I wanted to do was make it to the bed and commence my power nap as quickly as possible. And while my body was more than ready to shut down, my mind and spirit did not want to oblige. During the entire four-and-a-half hour drive to Indianapolis, I sensed an odd heaviness I could not shake off or explain. Emotionally, I felt as dreary as the rain soaked streets. I prayed nearly the whole way down, but I still could not understand where this feeling was coming from. I had no reason to be sad, aside from the need to leave my family one more time. What made it even more confusing was that this did not feel like a normal sadness. The best way I could describe it would be to say that I was sensing *someone else's* sadness. I asked the Lord if this was coming from Him and got nothing back. Resigned to having no answer, I fell into bed and forced myself to sleep.

The 4:00 A.M. alarm was a joyous sound. I rolled out of bed pretty much angry at the world and with only a few minutes to clear my head before jumping into the shower. I took a deep breath and headed over to the in-room coffee maker for a much needed pick me up. As the java began to brew, I noticed something troubling on my spirit. The sadness was still there and it was stronger than ever. Now at my wits end, I knelt down beside the bed and cried out to God to show me what was wrong.

Instantly a very detailed and powerful vision formed in my mind's eye. There before me stood a little boy some distance away. He was small for his age with light brown hair. Though he was strong and healthy, in my vision he seemed very unsure and vulnerable. As if he sensed this, I could tell the boy was straining to be strong and mature. His eyes locked on mine. His gaze spoke a million words, though he made no sound. He stood there waiting expectantly, clutching a small stuffed Snoopy doll. The second my eyes spotted that doll I recognized the child. It was my younger self, from almost 30 years earlier. To my shock and horror, I realized he had been waiting for someone to find him all this time…

REWIND

That child was born on February 19, 1971. And while I could say I was born a poor child while Elvis Presley is heard singing *In the Ghetto* in the background, I do not want to give the impression of a life of tremendous struggle or great obstacles. As a matter of fact, I consider myself a child of privilege. I always knew I was loved, accepted, safe and secure. I never went without food, shelter or shoes. I wanted for nothing. Of course being young, I had nothing to compare it against, so to me it was perfect.

Then there was the factual side. My parents loved each other very much. That love manifested itself in a pregnancy before they were married. I believe they intended to get married someday, but certainly not so soon. Mom was seventeen, Dad was nineteen. I am grateful they chose to do the "honorable" thing. I do not think that was ever in doubt. And nine months later we were a family, a family that had little more than the love between Mom and Dad, but had now expanded to include a baby boy.

Dad left college after his first year. Mom finished high school early, and we moved into a tiny duplex near my grandparents in downtown Indianapolis. The neighborhood was not great, but all of our family was close by and nothing was beyond walking distance. Everything we had was hand-me-down—clothes, furniture, dishes. That was how things worked in an extended family with strong bonds but little money. Dad worked two jobs. Mom got a job as well. Dad borrowed money from Grandpa to buy an old, used Plymouth Roadrunner. Mom and Dad became so good at saving they could stretch a penny into copper wire. We lived simply but happily. We could not do a whole lot, but families did not do that much anyway in those days. Mom and Dad sacrificed greatly to get this new family off the ground. And they were very committed to loving me unconditionally and providing me with a comfortable life.

THE BOY GETS HIS NAME

During my early years, Mom, Dad and I formed a really tight unit. It was just the three of us—the three amigos. I think because they were so young, and fairly clueless on how to parent, they treated me as an adult from day one. I am not saying they put some crazy undue pressure on me or stole my childhood. On the contrary, they simply allowed me to grow into a loving friendship with them, based on mutual respect. I did not know any better, so it worked for me. I can remember my mom telling me that by the time I was two, the family had nicknamed me "little man," because I acted so mature. In the mind of a toddler, that is high praise. All a child wants when he is little is to be like his parents, so I embraced my new moniker with gusto. As I got older, I reveled in comments like, "You're so mature," and "Chris acts so grown up for his age." I know my parents appreciated it too.

Maturity was kind of the overriding culture of our family. Both Mom and Dad were raised in fairly structured environments. My grandparents, having lived through the Depression and a world war, were very practical and emotionally tough. This upbringing made my dad quite logical and emotionally detached and my Mom very stoic and "matter of fact." This may not sound like a warm or caring combination, but my parents were very warm and caring. They simply made it abundantly clear that certain behaviors were expected. I remember treating it like a game. I would try to see how mature I could be and then watch what kind of reaction I could get. I would listen to the adults talk and try to recite the biggest words in my own conversations. Any reaction was great, but if I could get a laugh too, I was in heaven. I was really in my glory when I got my first suit. It was for my aunt's wedding, and man, was it sweet. Picture a five-year-old in a powder blue, three-piece with big dark blue buttons and pin striping. Don't laugh, it was the 70's! I remember swinging the jacket over my shoulder, looking like a JC Penney's catalogue model. I loved that suit. I was little man head to toe. Everybody, of course, agreed.

Validation like that was all I needed. I developed a very strong urge to please and to never be a burden. Sure, there were many times when I messed up and got into trouble. That was usually when I would hear Dad tell me to use my head for more than a hat rack. He often corrected with humor and sarcasm, which compelled me to include even these altercations into my own repertoire. But I strived to be self-disciplined, and I would sooner die than hear my dad say, "I'm disappointed in you." This was the harshest rebuke I could get from him, thus something to be avoided at all costs. As long as I did that, life was smooth and my image flourished.

Maturity Tested

Because Mom and Dad both had to work, something had to be done with me during the day. My aunt watched me for a while, but I think she ended up going to work as well. Since most everyone in the family was working, the only option was to pay a babysitter—somebody we did not know. Definitely somebody I did not know. It is difficult to recall those first few babysitters. I do remember feeling scared and uncertain whenever Mom would drop me off. It was during this time that I switched from acting emotionally mature to being emotionally mature.

Now it was for real. I learned quickly to push down the fear and uncertainty. I reasoned that I had to be mature and that my feelings did not matter. I wanted to be the "little man." I had to suck it up and go with the flow. I am sure Mom and Dad would have preferred not to leave me with strangers, but if they did not have a choice, neither did I. We were the three amigos, right? They were counting on me and I was not about to let them down. I do not think I ever complained, even through a lot of interesting situations and questionable households. To be sure, it was a lot for a little kid to face all alone. Yet, even at this young age, I developed a deep sense of obligation. Instead of merely seeking childish validation, I now had a real reason to act like a grown-up.

Do not get me wrong; the places I stayed were not abusive or dangerous. Nothing happened that was particularly tragic or emotionally damaging. There was a simple reality, however, that on the lower, middle-class neighborhood streets, things happened that were less than positive. That may not be a shocking statement, but as a little kid facing it alone, I had to make some choices. If I got into a scrape, I had to fight or flee, and learn pretty quickly when to do which. If I got teased, I could take it or tease back. I usually chose the latter. I could be a loner or force myself to make friends. Slowly I began to figure out that the little man approach seemed to be the ticket.

Acting mature accomplished a lot of things. For one thing, it endeared me to adults responsible for my care. I could act up like the rest of the kids, but I was typically the last one to get in trouble. If I did get in trouble, a quick joke or a sentence of big words could get me out of it. The quick wit, humor and vocabulary I had picked up from my dad helped me in other ways too. If a bigger kid was threatening to beat me up, I tried to make him laugh and pull him to my side. I got really good at this because nearly every kid I knew was bigger than me. The down side was that once most of the big kids were on my side, I became cocky and started using my humor to make fun of others. Sadly, I got good at this too.

Still, there were times where my emotions got the better of me. Anticipation would well up inside my stomach everyday about five o'clock. I remember vividly how that anticipation would quickly turn to anxiety as the five o'clock hour would begin to pass. It was the worst when Mom was more than a few minutes late. The winter time was even more difficult because it would start getting dark about then. Occasionally, I would have to stuff down tears as I waited expectantly by the front door.

I can still feel the panic of wondering where Mom was, questioning why she had not come. It may have only been a half an hour or 45 minutes. But to me, it was an eternity. I guess it is pretty typical for a child to react that way, and my parents tried their best to reassure me. Every time it happened I vowed to get more mature. I swore to myself that the tears and the panic would never happen again. Sure enough, it happened less and less. I took pride in the fact that I could handle the situation, but even more pride that I could control my emotions.

TGIF

Weekends were the best. I was always much more excited to get picked up on Friday than any other day. Friday marked the start of two days dedicated to the three amigos. Mom and Dad did not have to work. I did not have to go to the babysitter. We were not an "on the go" type of family, so we spent a lot of time just hanging out. Friday nights were eat out night. Mom, Dad and I would go out for a nice dinner, usually somewhere like McDonald's or Burger Chef. If we really went fancy, it would be an all-you-can-eat steak house like Ponderosa or Bonanza. Hey, I said we did not have much! Besides, fast food is five-star for a six-year-old. On a side note: Mom said one of my first words was "fi-fies."

After that, they would take me over to Grandma and Grandpa's house to spend the night. I guess Mom and Dad used it as their date night, but I did not care. This was all about me. I loved spending the night at Grandma's. She even gave me a special overnight bag to use. It was shaped like a giant basketball shoe. I would pack it with all the essentials: underwear, socks, jammies and, oh yes, that bean-bag Snoopy dog, also a gift from her. That dog was my favorite and I carried it with me everywhere. I would walk in, throw my little shoe bag on the floor and jump on the couch to watch "Dukes of Hazzard" and the "Incredible Hulk." Yeeeee-haw! Sometimes I would sit with Grandpa in his big old recliner. He and I would draw pictures for each other while he would tell stories from the war. In the morning, Grandma would get up early and I would go crawl in bed with him. We would talk about anything and everything while Grandma got breakfast ready. I was safe, comfortable and without a care in the world. If Norman Rockwell were here, he would have painted this.

Saturdays at the house were for doing yard work and watching football. If staying around home was not on the agenda, I would usually tag along while Mom and Dad went shopping, or played tennis, or whatever. It did not matter to me as long as we were all together. Plus, they always had someone on hand to "drive" the cart or be the ball boy.

We did not split up much, but if we did, it was probably because Dad took me to the gym while he played basketball. I loved going to the gym. It was back in the old neighborhood, and it was a true "old school" building. My cousins and I would run all over that place while our dads faced "all comers" in pick up games. My only regret is that I did not watch Dad play more during those days. He was truly gifted on the court. I still hear stories about what he could do with a basketball. It was not until recently that I found out he had been invited to try out by some of the Indiana Pacers players. Remember how I talked about sacrifices?

Anyway, on Sundays, Dad's whole side of the family would gather back at Grandma's house and she would make lunch. It was always a full tilt "grandma" meal: fried chicken, green beans, macaroni and cheese, biscuits and sweet iced tea. Sundays at Grandma's was the closest thing we had to a weekly prayer meeting, no prayer included. Grandma was really flexible too. You could show up and eat any time, as long as it was 12:00 noon. In her own sweet, very passive/aggressive way, Grandma ran a tight ship. She was definitely the matriarch of the family. As I got older, I also realized that she had a strong faith in Jesus Christ. But oddly enough, that was not something she imposed on the rest of the family, at least not by the time I came along. None the less, those Sundays were filled with love, laughter and a sense of togetherness that I came to cherish.

NOT EVEN CHR-EASTER

The holidays were another time of great importance in my life. They were like a bunch of Sundays jammed together at one time. I got a big dose of family and an even bigger dose of Mom and Dad. We did the usual stuff. At Thanksgiving, we gathered at Grandma's house, of course. And, of course it was always at 12:00 noon. But instead of the usual Sunday menu, we had turkey, dressing and all the trimmings. It was also a time when the whole family gathered, not just those closest by. Dad's side of the family is not huge. He has two sisters who each have kids of their own. I have four cousins, three of which were boys at least a few years older. I loved getting to see them, but I did have to endure my share of wedgies and Indian burns.

Like most families we would split time on Thanksgiving and visit both sides. Later in the afternoon we would leave Dad's parents and head to one of Mom's siblings or aunt's houses. Mom's side of the family was a lot different. To begin with, it was a lot bigger. Mom was born in the middle of a run of six kids. Her mom had a big family as well. So, by the time we added in the cousins, second cousins and great aunts, Thanksgiving was a big "do," as Mom would say. It looked like a church pot-luck. The dinner was about twelve different dishes with three or four pans of each dish. It was a lot more food than anyone could possibly eat. The house was always chaotic—kids running everywhere, people saying "hi" whose names I could never remember. It was fun and warm, but different. Most of Mom's side had chosen to stay with their independent Baptist upbringing, so these family events had a much more religious tone. It was not what I was used to, but I was never uncomfortable. The next holiday was a different story.

Mom's side of the family did not celebrate Christmas. Obviously, they chose to honor God in their own way by not following the seasonal traditions, but growing up, I did not understand it. I thought it was…well… weird. How could you not celebrate Christmas? It was the greatest time of the year. I loved every part of it, at least the parts I was exposed to. The tree, the presents, the candy, the TV specials, the decorations: what's not to love? To me it was all great. And the whole reason for the season? Well, for me that never came into the picture.

The season kicked off with the typical hunt for a Christmas tree. Mom, Dad and I would spend hours driving around to parking lots and hardware stores, looking for that perfect specimen. Standing in the slush and cursing the cold, we would joke about the ones that leaned to one side and laugh at the look-alikes of the sad little tree in the *Charlie Brown* Christmas cartoon. Finding one we all agreed on, we would cut it down. Not quite…I mean we would pull it out of the stand, pay for it, stuff it in the back of Mom's Chevy Nova and drive it home.

The smell of pine would fill our small house as I waited anxiously for the tree to open. Then we could hang those great multi-colored, big bulb lights on it along with some sweet, oversized 1970s ornaments. Oh, and *Charlie Brown?* I never missed him or any of the other Christmas specials. I would sprint from anywhere in the house when I heard that CBS jingle announcing a special program on the TV.

I loved to help Grandma decorate her tree as well. She had boxes and boxes of really old ornaments. I played with them for hours and thought how cool it was that my dad had played with them too when he was my age. Like Thanksgiving, the family would gather at her house on Christmas Eve. Christmas Eve was better, because there were presents, and lots of them. Gift opening time was ridiculous. The whole family would jam into the tiny front room, made even smaller by the oversized evergreen and scores of neatly wrapped boxes. By the time paper started flying, it was over a hundred degrees and any order or process was quickly lost. Luckily, we had already taken care of the mandatory family pictures in front of the tree. By the end, you could not see the floor from all the torn paper, ribbons and discarded packaging. This was my heaven. I would spend the rest of the evening playing with whatever I had gotten, laughing, joking and reveling in the fact there was more to come in the morning.

What was not coming in the morning was a trip to church. Mom, Dad and I would wake up early, really early, open presents and have breakfast. It was perfect. It was the three amigos. I had their undivided attention and a bunch of new stuff to play with. If I got a train set, Dad would help me set it up. If I got a set of connecting blocks, Dad would build with me. That's all I needed. I had no clue there was anything more; any deeper meaning to the holidays. Easter was the same. We simply inserted baskets, eggs and candy for trees, lights and ornaments. And, we inserted it all in the place of God and Jesus. We had family. We had each other. We had time together. That was very important. It was the most important. It is a good thing that it was all I needed, because it was all I had.

Chapter Two

A Gift Unwrapped

"But Jesus called the children to him and said,
"Let the little children come to me, and do not hinder them, for the
kingdom of God belongs to such as these.""

LUKE 18:16

ALL ON MY OWN

If anything was missing, I could not name it. Once I had sufficiently learned how to swallow the fear and other emotions, my life was in cruise control. Besides, it wasn't like I had a choice. Mom and Dad both had to work, so I had to do my part. If that meant not seeing them as much as I wanted to, so be it. Even at this young age, I understood the importance of sacrificing to keep things copasetic. And I was committed to maintaining the picture of maturity. Getting upset, or as my Dad termed it, "lapsing into chaos" was something he frowned upon, so that was out. Except in extreme cases, the little man kept his composure.

A good example of this is the time I tried to walk home from soccer practice. I played in a community soccer league from about 8 to 11 years old. During my first or second season, we practiced at a junior high school on the outskirts of our township. On this particular day, my parents dropped me off for practice and left as they normally did. Well, for some reason, the practice ended early and everyone else went home with their parents. While waiting outside the school, I started thinking it could be a long time before Mom and Dad arrived. This realization did not scare me, but it did make me impatient. So instead of continuing to wait, I decided to walk home. It seemed perfectly logical to me, but in reality the school was at least five miles from our house; over the freeway, near Thirtieth Street. We lived off of Tenth Street. I remember walking for a long time and wondering why I had not made it very far. The trip definitely seemed quicker in the car. After walking a bit further, it suddenly dawned on me that my parents would get to the school and not know where I had gone. I do not remember if I turned around and walked back or if somebody picked me up, but in my mind, I had it all under control.

In spite of these occasional fits of "logic," my little man persona won me the opportunity to be a latchkey kid by the fourth grade. My parents felt I was mature enough to stay at home by myself after school. I loved it. No more odd babysitters. No more waiting in strange places for Mom or Dad to come and get me. If I had to be alone, being at home alone was much better. I had freedom to roam the neighborhood, or stay around the house. It did not matter that I got teased at school for actually having a key around my neck. It felt a sense of independence that fueled my desire to be mature. It was validation in the purest sense. Whether or not Mom and Dad had that in mind when they made the decision did not matter. I embraced the chance to show I could take care of myself. My parents only had a few guidelines: do your homework, get the grass mowed, do not let anybody in the house, simple things like that.

With exception of a few bouts of forgetfulness and procrastination, I made sure to finish my chores before Mom and Dad got home. Once those were out of the way, I had ample time to do all the stuff one would expect a young boy to do, especially one that was unsupervised. And whenever possible I preferred to do it in the company of neighborhood kids. Regardless of what we got into, the neighborhood pack and I never ceased trying to one-up each other. For instance, we would build ramps for our bikes and see how far and high we could jump. But that got old quickly. So we began to lay our bodies in front of the ramps to see how many people we could jump at one time. Now we were talking real danger. Yet we were fair about it as well. The guy on the end always got to be the next to jump. If someone did not clear the bodies and landed on him, he got to jump twice. We did what one would call normal stuff as well. Things like build forts or play football. Yet I recall laughing the hardest and having the most fun when there was a chance of getting hurt. I did not really get scared unless I thought something might get me in trouble. That was one thing I could not let happen.

REMAIN CALM, ALL IS WELL

On a few occasions, I locked myself out of the house. That got me scared. Not because I was locked out, but because I couldn't bear to disappoint my parents. This image flashed through my mind of me sitting on the front porch when my Mom pulled up, and my having to explain what happened. Then the conversation would take place between Mom and Dad where they might reconsider the responsibility they had given me. If it went really badly, I would hear those five words I still tried to avoid: "I'm very disappointed in you." I would rather have my father smack me upside the head than utter that phrase. It could destroy the little man's validation in the blink of an eye.

The first time I locked myself out, panic overwhelmed me. I had gone out through the front door and locked it behind me. After forcing myself to gather my wits, I figured I could find something slim enough to jimmy the lock. Don't ask me why I thought this. Maybe I saw it on an episode of S.W.A.T or Starsky and Hutch. For whatever reason, I was convinced it was my best chance to get in. The only problem was that I had nothing to act as a jimmy. Fourth graders do not carry credit cards. At least they did not back then.

I hunted around outside and eventually found something to pry the door open. I remember the sense of victory I felt once I was safely inside. Like so many other little battles I faced, I found a way to overcome without going to my parents. Anytime I could work through something without help, I counted it a success. I hated admitting I could not do something or that I needed help. As a result, I avoided things I could not master, and stuck with things that brought me praise like playing soccer and drawing. In my mind, I had a pretty well managed life for a ten-year-old. I relied on no one and needed very little. So I thought.

INVITATION

Then, that same year, something happened. My cousins invited me to a roller skating party. Nothing out of the ordinary about that, but the reason for the party was unusual. This was not for school or for a birthday party. This was a party sponsored by their church, a small independent Baptist church on the east side of Indianapolis. I agreed to go even though we were not members of the congregation. We were not members of any congregation, actually. My parents had grown up attending another Baptist church in the inner city, but after they got married and had me, they were not what could be called regular attendees. I could count the number of times the three of us were in church together on one hand. Nonetheless, I was cool with it. I had been to church with my cousins on a number of occasions, and it was always a pleasant experience—different, but pleasant. I did the vacation Bible school bit. I even had the hand-painted cross in my room to prove it. But church was never a place I connected with. I saw no reason to be there. I got the whole "Jesus Loves Me" story, but I did not understand my part in it. I certainly did not understand enough to know that I needed Him. I needed no one, remember? Most everything I needed in my life my parents gave me or I had figured out for myself. I was the little man; self sufficient, self-confident, self-contained. Where did God, Jesus and church fit in all of that?

While I was not sure on the whole God thing, I am sure I said yes because I did not want to miss a chance to get together with my cousins. In spite of the church tie in and the fact I had not mastered roller skating, hanging out with Joe and Jason was always a good time. We were the three musketeers. I was much closer with them than my buddies from the neighborhood. Joe was a year older than me, and Jason was a year younger. I fit right in, and they treated my like a brother. They were the closest thing I had to brothers. Whenever we got together, you could bet that there would be an adventure, a lot of noise, something possibly getting broken and a ton of laughter.

That night at the roller rink was no different. I mean, how can you not have fun at a roller rink? Bad food, bad skating, great games and cheesy music; it was a preteen's dream. Who remembers the *"Double-Dutch Bus"*?

Reverse skate? How about *"Rocket"* by Herbie Hancock? Oh yeah, and those sweet, flesh colored rental skates? Yes, I am so dating myself. But I don't care. It was one of those funky generational things I have to own up to. I apologize to those of you who are not from the skating party era. I remember pushing each other to see how much speed we could pick up, tripping each other and generally wreaking havoc. The funniest thing about the whole event was that, right in the midst of all the music and chaos, my younger cousin, Jason, came up to me and asked, "Hey, do you want to go get saved?" To which, I promptly responded: "Sure."

I'LL MEET YOU THERE

The innocence of the exchange was remarkable. Jason could have easily replaced the phrase "get saved" with "play foosball," and my response would have been the same. It was only by the grace of God that I happened to recall that getting saved meant asking Jesus into your heart, so I figured it could not hurt. I had no idea of the magnitude of what I was about to do. If I had realized, I am sure I would have come up with a clever reason to say no.

We bounded over to a circle of chairs next to the coat lockers, where the youth pastor was seated with a group of about four other boys. We joined hands and he led us in the prayer of salvation. As we prayed, I felt something I had never felt before. I felt warm inside and I sensed that someone else was there with me. The sensation should have been unsettling. I was only used to sensing myself. I liked that. I was comfortable with that. I prided myself on being in control of my emotions and closing everything else out. But this feeling was not uneasy or upsetting. It was peaceful, comforting, so I went with it.

When the pastor came to the part of the prayer about Jesus dying for us and repenting from our sin, I began to cry. *Whoa, hold on here,* I thought to myself. Now I was uneasy. Why was I crying? For one thing, I did not even have a full grasp of what sin was, and for another, I only cried when I got hurt—badly. Not to mention, I could catch a whole bunch of ribbing from Joe and Jason if they saw me cry. I know I would have done the same to them. We made a habit out of giving each other the business. So that fact, coupled with a lot of practice being the big boy, forced back the tears in most situations.

But this time was different. The pastor's words faded into the background as my mind raced to process what was happening. I began to argue with myself over this whole crying deal. At first I thought: *You're just making yourself cry because you think you're supposed to.* To which I replied: *Yeah right, you're supposed to cry in a crowded roller rink with people watching!* Even at this early age, I had mastered the art of the internal argument. If I had followed the usual pattern, I would have spun myself right out of the moment. But as I said, this time was markedly different. I felt a calmness stemming from the presence. I was convinced it was the Lord's presence. I sensed Him leading me to a place I had not been—a place I did not know existed. I realized I was not forcing myself to cry. I had a desire to cry coming from this place. It was a cry separate from my emotions. What little I could identify of my "spirit" was calling out to Jesus. I knew that my bad behavior kept me from God, and I wanted to be with Him.

The pastor's voice drifted back into the forefront of my mind. He came to the part in the prayer where I was supposed to ask Christ into my heart. As the words rolled off his lips, I remember everything else being drowned out. At the risk of being overly dramatic, it seemed as if time stopped, waiting for my response. The wait was not long. With childlike simplicity and innocence I said: "Jesus, come into my heart." And guess what? He came. With disco music blaring overhead, and people having fun all around, He met me there. In a most unlikely chain of events, I received the most important gift of my life. When it would have been so easy to say "no thanks," or to simply fake it, I actually made the decision to accept Jesus as my Savior. My life was changed forever. I knew something was different, but I had no idea what. I even found a keepsake to commemorate the event. I bought a key and lock set for a quarter in one of those trinket vending machines. I did not buy a rubber ball, or a set of wax lips. I bought a cheap little metal key and lock. I am not even sure why something so peculiar would be in a machine like that, but the significance of it would come back to me in later years.

It is hard to imagine a supernatural event happening at a USA Skate in

Indianapolis, Indiana, but that was exactly what took place. Nothing else could explain why I would joyfully and eagerly do something so "churchy" right in the middle of having a great time; not to mention the bizarre and truly miraculous orchestration of events that brought me to that point. The silliness of the whole afternoon makes me laugh to this day.

INTO THE JUNK DRAWER

So there I was, a new creation in Christ with my eternity secure, yet I had no clue what to do next. Since I was not raised in a church, I had nowhere to "plug in." I would like to say I knew to start proclaiming the good news to everyone, but I can't. As I said, I was not fully aware of the magnitude of the decision I had made. I did know *something* was different, but I could not articulate it. Telling my parents was pretty much the beginning and end of my proclamation. When I got home, the conversation went pretty much like this: "How was the skating party?" "Great, I got saved." (Insert chirping cricket sound effect). Needless to say, Mom and Dad were caught off guard. They looked at each other and looked back at me. I do not remember if they said anything, but if they did, it was equivalent to an "OK, great" from the movie *Wayne's World*. I am sure they were happy for me on some level, but at the same time, I know they had questions about what had actually happened.

Many times after that I myself questioned what happened. But I truly had no questions at that moment. Even if I had wanted to get more information, I would not have known how to ask for it. I quite literally didn't know what I didn't know. I had no one to come alongside me and say that this was the start of a journey not an end state. There was no one to speak about discipleship or growing closer to God. I do not remember if there was even a Bible in the house for me to start reading; not that I would have known to read it regularly anyway. A long time passed without the topic ever coming up again. My parents probably figured I had forgotten all about it. And I am sure they were relieved that I did not press the issue. I do not think what happened to me that day was at all offensive to them; it was just a place that they were not comfortable going.

I never quite knew what drove my parents from church life. We never talked about it. At least it was never talked about in front of me. Regardless of the reasons Mom and Dad left the church, their son's newfound faith was not enough to bring them back. This did not bother me, because as I said, I did not know any better. So, I put the Gift on a shelf, bow still in tact. The greatest treasure I had ever received remained unopened. I knew Jesus was in my heart, but I did not seek to know Him more. In all honesty, He was easy to pack away along with my emotions. Just like the key and locket I had purchased that night at the roller rink, I tossed my faith into the junk drawer of things forgotten. Yet I did not do this intentionally. I simply allowed my Salvation and resultant faith to follow the same pattern of other significant experiences in my life. I had gotten very good at leaving things behind, stuffing emotions down, sucking it up, toughing it out. Pick a cliché. That was what mature people did. It was what the little man did. And I reasoned that if my parents did not want to discuss it, there must not be a good reason to do so. The last thing I wanted to do was buck the system. I had a good thing going, and as always, I did not want to disappoint.

Moving On

Life was still pretty good. For the next four years, all was well. I finished elementary school. Mom and Dad kept working hard and saving every penny. They saved so well, we were able to build a much bigger house way out in the suburbs. It was corn country actually. I remember the first time we drove out to the lot where our new house was going to stand. The drive took only twenty minutes, but it may as well have been four hours. I kept watching cornfield after cornfield go by. The same word kept flashing through my mind: "Boonies" as in the boon docks. I even stretched it out for emphasis: "Booo-neees." I knew this was going to cramp my self-sufficient lifestyle. In the city, I could ride to all my friends' houses. I could ride to the mall and to my grandparents' house. I could ride everywhere. Now I realized my little one-speed Huffy dirt bike was not going to get me far in this great expanse. In addition to the concerns from the transportation/logistics department, I had the stress of trying to make new friends in a new school. But again, these were minor adjustments for the little man.

Mom and Dad were pretty stressed out about building a new house.

This was by far and away the biggest investment two young ghetto kids had ever made. You could take all of the houses and apartments we had lived in up to that point and set them inside this palatial estate. So if they were preoccupied with that, I had to carry my load. No disruptions. No boat rocking. Since I still felt there was nothing I could not handle, I would not allow this to trip me up. Everything was under control.

Chapter Three

The World Ends

"You boast, 'We have entered into a covenant with death, / with the grave /
we have made an agreement...we have made a lie our refuge
and falsehood our hiding place.'"

<small>ISAIAH 28:1</small>

NUKED

I awoke to a typical winter Saturday morning. Winters in the Midwest are brutal, especially in the months following Christmas. It is after the novelty of snow-filled holidays wears off that the really crappy weather seems to hit. I am not talking about a ton of nice fluffy powder like you see in Colorado or Buffalo. No, in Indiana, it was ice storms so heavy the trees bent over and touched the ground. Wind chill that seared our flesh and made our nose hairs stick together. If temperatures did manage to creep up, we got a string of cold, dark, rainy days that seem to run together forever. It was what I affectionately called "serial killer" weather.

It was that kind of morning in early February. February—man, if it weren't for the fact I was born in that month, I would call it a total write-off. Even the thought of my birthday brought little solace most years. So, having no desire to go outside, I settled in for the usual bowl of cereal and a morning full of cartoons. Before I could decide between Cocoa Puffs or Frankenberry, Dad came in and asked if I wanted to go with him to get doughnuts. Doughnuts instead of cereal? That was a no-brainer. I said

"OK" and jumped in the car. Dad and I had made the doughnut run a frequent weekend ritual. In the old neighborhood, we could actually walk to get them. Now it was about a half hour ride.

Light flurries began as we backed down the driveway. The stiff, icy wind drove the tiny flakes sideways through the air. I remember wanting the car to hurry up and get warm. As we left the subdivision and traveled a while, I noticed that the car was quiet. I do not think we even had the radio playing. Dad was quiet as well, but that was not out of the ordinary for him. He seldom spoke much, and he would say even less if he had a lot on his mind. I could tell he had a lot on his mind lately. After several more minutes, Dad awkwardly broke the silence and started to speak. He said something like: "Chief, I need to talk to you" or "tell you something." I do not remember the exact words he used, but he spoke quietly and very deliberately, never taking his eyes off the road. I could sense a torrent of emotions under his words as he began to slowly explain how he and Mom were not getting along. He painstakingly stated that they needed some time apart to work things out. Even though Dad wasn't looking at me, I cannot forget the look in his eyes. They were glassy, distant. It was as if he could not believe what was coming out of his own mouth.

Of course, I could say I couldn't believe it either, but I was not yet to that point. It was as if the words had not even begun to register in my mind. Dad continued. He told me that it was not Mom's fault, and it was not anything I had done either. He asked me not to be mad and he pleaded with me to not blame her or myself. He said he would be moving out for a while, but not to worry because we would still see each other a lot.

DAZED AND CONFUSED

Don't get mad and don't worry? The truth is I did not know what to do. At this point, I still had no clue what to get mad or worried about. Dad's words were cryptic, yet so matter of fact, I resorted to merely following along. I remember them banging around in my head without settling on any particular thought or emotion. The magnitude of what was happening was nowhere close to sinking in. To this day, I am not sure if I was in total shock, or if I had truly become that adept at cutting off my emotions. Unfortunately, I suspect it was the latter. But it happened so subtly and easily there was no way I could catch myself or even realize it was happening.

You know how things seem to move in slow motion when you get really bad news? Your vision gets narrow and your chest tightens up. It is almost like a fight or flight response. I did neither. I was stunned. None of the typical questions came. What? Why? How can this be happening to our family? If it is not my fault then whose fault is it? I felt like I was outside the car looking in; like it was not really me in that situation.

I do not recall what I said exactly, but I do know it was not much. I also know that my tendency to close off my emotions must have been kicking into overdrive. I did not cry. I did not get angry. I cannot say what kind of response Dad was expecting, but I definitely gave him little to go on. I quietly said, "OK," and began to immediately think about how I could be strong for Mom and Dad during this time. Be strong. Be tough. That tactic had worked well to this point in my life, so I knew I could use it to get me through this. I could be the mature kid and not be a burden to anyone. All I needed to do was keep my feelings out of it.

That was pretty much the end of the talk in the car. I think Dad spoke up again after a while and asked if I was okay. "Yeah, I'm fine," I replied. That would become my pat answer over the next few months.

Moving Out

I was still reeling from the shock of the "doughnut run" on the day I helped Dad move into his tiny apartment about twenty minutes away. We borrowed my grandpa's old Ford pick-up, loaded it with Dad's stuff and headed out. It felt like this was all he had in the world. When we pulled into the complex, a huge sense of "wrongness" overwhelmed me. Everything about this day seemed so wrong. But that was as far as I let the feeling go. I shook it off, jumped out of the truck and started to unload.

The apartment was dark, stuffy and old. The air was stale and dank. Everything might as well have been covered with that groovy brown paneling. The carpets looked like they had been "cleaned" but still looked a hundred years old. Given the circumstances, it was probably appropriate, but I could not imagine living there, especially by myself.

I vividly remember hauling stuff in and haphazardly stacking it anywhere there was space. Even though the apartment was small, it looked vast and empty. Dad had very little to put in it. With as much as I would allow myself to feel, I felt sorry for him. I could not understand why he was doing this. Why would he want to be alone in a lonely place? What made it worse was the sense that he did not understand it either. I did my best to stay disengaged, but I could still pick up that he seemed to be as confused and uncertain as I was. At this point, my disbelief drifted into denial. I refused to believe this could be happening in our lives. It felt like a bad, bad dream, or some cheesy made-for-TV drama. It had to be… Nothing about the situation made any sense. So rather than trying to make sense of it or dealing with these thoughts, I shut my mind down and went through the motions.

The fact that my mind could not deal made it all the easier to keep my heart in check. Any sadness or hurt that crept up was quickly clamped down. If I did not cry when Dad dropped the bomb on me in the car, I certainly was not going to cry about it now. I was numb. I do not recall feeling much of anything. I reassured myself that my feelings were not important. I tried to make sure Dad had what he needed, even though I did not know what that was. We finished moving his things and he dropped me off back at home. I cannot remember if I ever set foot back in that apartment. Not too long after that day, Dad moved back into our house.

Warning Signs

The next few months were interesting. I guess I hoped that things would get back to normal. Who wouldn't? In some respects they were normal— normal but not healthy. Dad and I did not see each other much or talk much. Mom and Dad seemed to have few conversations as well. In hindsight, I could see that it had been like that for a long time in our family. Really, it had been ever since we moved into the new house. I did not notice it was happening. As usual, I was wrapped up in what I had to do. I had to change schools, leave my friends, and adjust to a new neighborhood, all while transitioning from junior high to high school.

None of these things was particularly traumatic, but they contributed to a lack of awareness that the "three amigos" were drifting apart. Dad and I could go a whole week without exchanging more than a few sentences. Most of the time the three of us did spend together was in front of the TV. While this used to be fun, it now just seemed to be. I know that family dynamics and relationships change as kids get older and more involved in other activities, but when there is little emotion or communication in a family to begin with, many important things tend to get left unsaid.

This was clearly the case between Mom and Dad. Though I did not know it at the time, Dad had become restless and found comfort with another woman. I cannot tell you why or how, but it was something that the extended family picked up on long before I did. Several weeks before Dad told me what was going on, my older cousin, Jeff, took me aside and asked me if my parents were "doing okay." It seemed like such an odd question, I did not even know how to respond. I think I said, "They're doing fine." Jeff chose not to press the issue and I left it at that. It did not even occur to me to say, "Why do you ask?" I could have realized he knew something I did not know. I should have understood the reason he might ask that, given the fact that he saw his own mom go through two divorces. But similarly to the lack of communication, I did not pick up on this either. It seemed impossible that Mom and Dad could ever have problems. Now the impossible had become reality.

Dad's other relationship did not end when he moved back home. And, I am sure that was contrary to Mom's hope or expectation. They did try to work things out, I guess. I remember a few nights where I stayed at home while Mom and Dad met somewhere to talk. They seldom, if ever, discussed anything in front of me. They were so civil to each other it was hard to get a grip on what was really happening.

Finally, Mom told me one night that she had given Dad a choice. The pain and frustration broke through her tough exterior as she explained how she told Dad that he could not live both lives. He needed to decide who he wanted to be with. Dad made the choice, and moved out for the last time. Mom and Dad signed the papers, and before my fifteenth birthday, the marriage was over.

THE VOW

When Dad moved out the second time, I think I reacted even less than the first, though that may not seem possible. My efforts to keep a stiff upper lip and be mature during this time had been almost entirely successful. Almost. The main reason I was able to react so little when the divorce became final is because I had a chance to get everything out of my system previously. And I don't mean in a good way.

It all happened one night while Dad was back living with us. In one of the few discussions we actually had as a family during this time, the rather innocuous topic of Dad's Mercedes came up. I am a car guy, so allow me a brief pause to talk about this car. It was a beautiful, classic 1970 280 SL hardtop convertible. It was fully restored and it ran like a top. It had been in the family for a number of years. I was with Dad when he found it and bought it. The car only had two seats, but there was a space behind them big enough for me to sit in while he and Mom would cruise around town with the top removed. I loved that car.

For various reasons, the conversation came to a point where Dad said he would have to sell the Mercedes. "What!" I exclaimed. I was instantly horrified. This was the proverbial straw that broke the camel's back. In a reaction totally out of place for the situation, I lost it. I looked Mom straight in the eyes and yelled "This family is going to hell!" Then I stomped down the hall and slammed my bedroom door behind me. Discussion over.

Obviously the car was probably the last thing I was mad about. But it did not matter. At that point I was done. Safely locked in my dark room, I slumped down at the foot of my bed and began to weep heavily. I was so angry I could not control myself. And that loss of control only fueled my rage. All the hurt and confusion and fear and frustration came pouring out as I tried desperately to stop my sobs. Instead of letting it come, I railed against it. My anger grew. I slowly gathered my wits and started to focus my anger. *If this is how marriage goes,* I thought, *then forget it! I'll never get married.* What happened next was even more damning. Through clenched teeth I said in a low, bitter voice: "I'll never love anyone again if this is what it gets me." With that statement, I regained control and took a deep breath. The crying subsided as a steely resolve settled over me.

Suddenly I felt validated. A light bulb went off in my head. I remembered my little man persona from years ago and realized that was the way to go. I could bring it forward to fortify the angry young teen. All the things I had practiced through the years would pay off big time. Be mature. Do not show emotion. Stuff it down. Keep your heart out of it. That was it! At that moment, I rededicated myself to a heartless existence. Sincerity, compassion, caring—I could fake those. It began to feel kind of noble. Make sure everybody else is taken care of, but do not sweat your own feelings. That definitely made the most sense.

COMFORTABLY NUMB

From then on little man took over in a big way. I did my best to help Mom cope. I made sure Dad knew that I supported him. If anybody else in the family had concerns or questions, I reassured them. I definitely wanted everyone to know I was "OK." I could see the genuine concern in my friends and family during this time. They asked me repeatedly if I was feeling all right and if I needed to talk. My consistent answer was "I'm feeling fine; I don't need to talk." Even when pressed, the deepest I would go was only to say that I wanted Mom and Dad to be happy.

My behaviors and responses to the requests to help were so cool, calm and collected that the people who had asked were left bewildered. "Are you sure?" they would ask incredulously. I assume most of them figured I was not ready to talk about things, and that may have been some of it. But in reality, those that knew me best had come to expect this type of reaction. "Chris seems to be taking it well," I heard them frequently say. This directly validated my decision and justified my approach. The longer I persisted, the easier it got. In time, I came to a place where I could not have spoken to my feelings even if I had wanted to. I knew they were still there, but I was so out of touch I could not begin to express them. I no longer had to consciously stuff down anger or hurt or sadness. It was more like the connection to those emotions was severed. Staying mature and in control was becoming very easy—too easy.

It actually became like a game to me. Even though keeping my emotions in check had grown very simple, I was a smart enough kid to realize that I still had to proactively give them an outlet or deaden them. I gravitated toward things I knew would make me "feel" better or feel nothing at all. Some of these things were positive, some not so much. I liked riding my bike, so I spent a lot time out on the roads. During the summer before my freshman year, I would ride fifty or sixty miles a day. I would leave the house in the morning and not come home until dark. I did this partly just to get away, but also because a bike was my only mode of transportation. Remember we lived in the boonies, so all of my friends lived miles away. A group of us would get together at a buddies pool or ride up to the mall. I did not care as long as I was out of the house.

Riding was freedom, but it was also a great way to release aggression. I could ride as hard and fast as I wanted. I could get mad and curse the wind, and I did that a lot. I also used my bike to sneak and do things I shouldn't have. Things like: raiding the liquor cabinet, stuffing a gym bag full of booze and biking over to my friend's house to get drunk. At fourteen, I discovered that alcohol added a great dimension to blowing off steam and forgetting about life; thus started a long-standing relationship between abusing it and having fun.

On a less destructive note, music for me was another great way to release aggression. I was really into it. I grew up with Mom and Dad playing records or the radio while working around the house or driving in the car. I inherited their old stereo by the time I was eight or nine. It was quadraphonic! That means it had four speakers. And it also had a turntable and an eight track player. My older cousins turned me onto the hard rock scene, and I took to it like a fly to poop. For getting out aggression, you cannot beat cranking up AC/DC, Def Leppard, Van Halen, Styx or Kiss. I would sit in my room for hours and listen to them wail about living fast, partying hard and thumbing your nose at everything else. It sounded great to me.

Other than riding, drinking and blowing out my eardrums, my life was pretty sedate. I did the usual teenage stuff. I stayed up too late, ate too much junk food and watched way too much TV. The fact is I simply did not care. I did not care about myself or what I did. Anything that could take my mind off everything was good for me. And my heart? Well, that that was all but forgotten.

HELPLESS FOR MOM

The problem with not caring about yourself is that you tend to stop caring about anything or anybody. As the months wore on, I made less and less of an effort to make sure everyone else was alright. I grew cold and distant. Sure I still faked it. But as is typical, I let my guard down with the ones that were closest to me. The one closest to me in this new fractured family was Mom. Do not get me wrong, I am not saying I let my guard down enough to open up to her and share my true feelings. No, it was quite the opposite. I basically gave up trying to be "fine" around her. I was moody, argumentative, sarcastic, and that was when I bothered to say anything at all. For the most part, I just checked out.

Even if I had wanted to be honest and open with her, I am not sure I would have known what to say. Things were so different. Understandably, we were both in a state of shock. I could not imagine what she must have been feeling. It was now only the two of us in this big new house in the 'burbs. The person she expected to spend the rest of her life with left to be with someone else. I know she felt hurt, sad, confused, mad and frightened. Who wouldn't feel that way? The problem with Mom was that I could not tell. She appeared so strong and emotionally tough that these feelings rarely surfaced. She may have been acting that way for my sake, but one would not know because she acted that way about everything. Her approach to life was to "make do" and get on with it. And, for the most part, that is exactly what she did.

Sure, there were times when she struggled. For a while she did not sleep well. I got the impression that most mornings she used every ounce of strength she had just to pull herself out of bed. Yet she did not seem to allow herself the luxury of mourning for long. It may not have been much of a life initially, but she did get on with it. She would frequently join me for a mindless evening of TV. She dutifully hauled me back and forth to my friends, and to the mall. She kept up the house, cooked the meals— generally made my life as comfortable as possible. I wish I could say I did the same for her, but at the time I had very little to give.

She let me off the hook in those days. Her strength and stoic personality made it very easy for me to simply exist. She required very little of me, and I gave barely that. I just wanted to live my own life, and she honored my wish. We carved out our own spaces in that big, empty house and began to merely cohabitate. Honestly, it was not a cold or loveless existence. I think Mom knew where I was much better than I did, and she respected my desire for space. She did the best to love me the way she felt I needed to be loved. I am grateful to her for that. The only downside was that this lifestyle entrenched my belief that being closed off was the way to go.

Chapter Four

Living the Vow

"They are darkened in their understanding and separated from the life of God because of the ignorance that is in them due to the hardening of their hearts."

EPHESIANS 4:18

DOWN IN A HOLE

My freshman year of high school was kind of a blur. Even though I had found a lot of things to numb my heart, I still was not ready to make the jump from the little pond to the big one. I had a tough time adjusting. Lunchtime was a great example. Instead of going to lunch in groups, like in middle school, we were now released to go on our own. For some reason, I felt very uncomfortable going to the lunch room by myself. Even though I knew at least a few friends would be there, I did not want the exposure of finding a place to sit. The entire first semester that year my lunch consisted of a can of Pepsi, a bag of Munchos, and a Snickers Bar. Everything a growing boy needs, right? I would grab this bountiful feast out of the vending machines and sit against the wall of the gym by myself. Of course, it looked kind of cool and rebellious to eat junk food for lunch, and a lot of kids did it. For me, it was an odd kind of fear. Next to the gym, I felt less vulnerable and more anonymous. I did not want to talk to anyone about anything. The more invisible I could be the better.

I would not admit it, but the divorce affected me much more deeply than I could grasp. I now had a slew of new emotions to stuff down and control. The effort consumed me. I began to withdraw from my middle school running buddies. I would still go to the occasional party or hang out at the mall. But overall I had very little desire to socialize, so I quit reaching out to them and they eventually left me alone. Alone was exactly what I wanted to be. Sometimes. In reality, a strange paradox developed in my life. I felt like I needed to be around people, but being alone was easier. This constant clash of wants and needs usually resulted in my doing nothing. And, I got the chance to do that quite a bit, especially on the weekends.

Unlike me, Mom had made a decision to get on with her life. She started going out with friends and dating, which left me home by myself on Friday and Saturday nights. I did not mind the alone part, but the boredom was excruciating. With nothing to do and nowhere to go, my addiction to TV continued to grow. Do you remember when the TV stations would actually sign off for the night and play the National Anthem? I saw that more times than I would care to count. On school nights it was worse because I dreaded going back the next day. I would stay up until about 2:00 A.M. watching TV in my room, then roll out of bed at 6:00 A.M. the next morning to catch the bus or a ride with a friend.

Since I was eating and sleeping so well, one can imagine how my body responded. I developed a slight form of hypoglycemia. My blood sugar would tank and I would get serious dizzy spells. I could not eat anything in the morning. My stomach was always in knots, so anything I did eat for breakfast usually came right back up. I struggled to stay awake in class and would crash as soon as I got home from school. I had no energy to ride my bike, or study, or mow the grass, or clean my room. I definitely had no energy to engage emotionally. In those early days of high school, existing was about all I could muster.

I Got the Music in Me

I wish I had a better explanation as to what brought me out of my funk. I would love to say I got so tired of being isolated that I made the conscious choice to shake out of it. Better yet, it would be great to say that I turned toward God in my loneliest hour. But that was not the case. Actually, it was a number of things. Not the least of which, was the fairer sex. Even though at times I wanted to go unnoticed, my sense of humor and nonchalant attitude caused a few girls to look my way. And not just any girls—these were older girls. I learned years earlier that acting mature had a positive effect on the ladies, so who was I to keep it from paying dividends now? As I looked around more and more, I realized that this new environment offered many, new, smiling, pretty faces to enjoy. And the fact that several were smiling at me gave me a great boost of confidence. I started thinking that this high school thing might be kind of fun.

An even bigger boost of confidence came when a few buddies from school asked if I wanted to be in a band. We talked about it over the summer, and somehow they got the impression I could play the drums. Probably because I told them I could. Truthfully, I had never played before, but I was sure I knew how, so I said yes. In a leap of faith, I jumped from "air drumming" along with records to doing the real thing overnight. Dad and I split the price of an old used drum kit and I started playing with no lessons. Strangely enough, I was actually pretty good and I caught on quickly. It helped that I had a natural sense of rhythm and a lot of pent up aggression. When playing rock and roll, a person does not need much else.

Still, I was amazed by how comfortable I felt behind the drum set. It was as if I always knew how to play. Comfort led to passion and I began practicing as much as I could. Early on we rehearsed at one of the guitarist's houses and I hated it. I either had to haul my drums back and forth or leave them there. Eventually, I talked Mom into letting us practice at our house. The front room was empty from the divorce, so that became our rehearsal space. Out of courtesy, we would cover everything up with bed sheets when we were done, but it still looked odd. I do not think Mom cared, and I loved it. Now I could jam with the band or by myself whenever I wanted, or at least when Mom was gone. It was about the only thing in my life that felt real at the time. I got lost for hours in the simplicity and precision of the rhythms. I soothed my soul while banging out all my frustration. I would break sticks, cut my hands and sweat profusely, and the drums would always be ready for more. It was the closest I ever came to therapy. Honestly, if I had not discovered this gift, I would probably still be in therapy. And, yes, I now truly believe it was a gift, but at the time I did not think of it that way. At the time, I figured it was all me. I had no ability to acknowledge this gift, and certainly no consideration for a gift giver. All I knew was that it made me feel better, and it helped my cause in other areas.

Remember the girls that had looked my way? Well, they were looking more closely now. Once word got around that we had started a band, our stock went up significantly. I played the "rock star" role to the hilt. I started growing my hair out and wearing cut up concert tee-shirts. It did not matter that we never had any real gigs. We had great fun practicing and playing the parts. Plus, it was a great excuse to get together and drink. With all these new interests in my life, I started to develop a much more positive outlook. I was positive I could rely on music, girls and booze to keep me from feeling or caring. I now had nearly everything lined up for a sweet life.

Drive Time

Part of what drove me crazy my first year of high school was that I could not drive at all. Most nights at home, I felt so trapped I wanted to climb the walls. If Mom was out doing her thing, I was stuck without my trusty chauffeur. Not that I had many places for her to take me initially, but things became tougher when my social life improved. I could not strap my drums on my back and ride my bike to practice. And I most definitely was not going to have Mom drive me to pick up an older girl for a date. Since the girls were older, they usually were kind enough to drive, but that was beside the point. It cramped my style. Yep, this was definitely a missing piece to the puzzle—a very big piece.

I know most kids think their lives stink in those agonizing months before getting their licenses, but for a kid who prided himself on being independent and self sufficient, it was hell on earth. I desperately wanted to take off whenever I felt the urge. I craved the freedom of being able to come and go as I pleased. So much so that I took the car out a few times before I had my license and then lied to cover it up. Even the groundings from these episodes did not deter me from my belief that a car meant liberty. I was certain that was what I would have. And I was right.

A month after my sixteenth birthday, I had my license and the keys to my dad's '78 Monte Carlo. It was not much of a car, but as I said, I am a car guy, so I have got to describe it. It was silver except for the primer gray on the left quarter panel. It had wire rims, white walls and a vinyl top. And to top it off, it had crushed red velour interior. For all I cared, it could have had shag carpet, because to me it was a magic carpet. It transported me anywhere I needed to go: to school and back, to my job, since I made a deal to get one, to parties and girlfriend's houses. I no longer had to bum for rides or ask someone to pick me up. Anytime things got complicated, I could hit the road. And I did that quite often. It did not matter where I went or how long I was gone. What mattered was finally having the power to go.

With this final piece in place, I was now free to live the life I wanted. Driving was simply an enabler, an added dimension to my escape. Where TV and music gave me an internal release, the car gave me direct access to the rest of the world. In this world, I could have a good time and not be hampered with pesky emotions or deep relationships. I lived in pursuit of my own gratification. Much of that gratification came from the confidence of not relying on anyone. Unfortunately, confidence soon turned to cockiness which fueled my lack of care for anyone. Of course I could make people think I cared. But this was usually a mechanism to deflect the conversation from me back onto them.

Even when I wanted to care I refused to show it. I simply could not risk speaking my true heart. I convinced myself that shallow was easy. I patterned my life around a simple set of rules. Stay up too late? Sleep in 'til noon. Drink too much? Eat something greasy. Feelings for a girl get too deep? Shut them down and move on. Tick a friend off or hurt his feelings? Get him to laugh it off or tell him to get over it. I did whatever was necessary to keep things light. The alternative was reality, and at this point I had worked too hard to let reality spoil the show.

HARD LIVING

Keeping things light worked for quite a while. And I realized pretty quickly that my non-caring attitude allowed for an interesting social life. My friends in the band and I hung out in a larger group of guys that all shared a similar desire to live a consequence free existence. We were always in search of the next party. If we could not find one, we made one. Wherever we went, the good times followed. One day we would find ourselves lounging around a buddy's pool drinking beer and eating fudgecicles. The next we would be pounding liquor in a parking lot before heading into a ball game. Yes, sadly enough, our activities usually had alcohol as a key ingredient. School night or weekend, it did not matter. We made a game of finding creative ways to get it, hide it and drink it. With this kind of behavior, one would expect that the law of averages would catch up with us eventually. It did. Thank God not tragically, but it did.

The first time we got busted, it was only for underage possession. The officer was kind enough to release us to our parents at the police station. There was a moment of tension when Nick's dad, whom we all feared and respected, asked if we could be left in jail overnight. I assume to teach us a lesson. It might have helped. As it was, we kept on seeking the good times undaunted. There would be a series of other brushes with law enforcement, including a couple of nights in the drunk-tank complete with strip searches and lovely orange jumpsuits. But even this did not seem to faze us. I actually asked if I could keep my "Property Of" county jail ensemble as a souvenir. The only hard part was seeing my dad's face when they walked me out of the cell in handcuffs. Still, the sting of disappointing him faded from my hardened heart quickly, and we all laughed about our legal troubles as if we were rebels without a clue.

Even without booze, this group of guys could find dumb stuff to do. We stole all the usual stuff: street signs, barricades, and lawn statues. We would liberate anything we could fit in the back of our cars. We also got creative with gun powder and coffee cans, power tools and spray paint. We would invent games involving high speed chases around the streets of Indianapolis, throwing various food items at each other's cars. It sounds crazy, but it was anything to pass the time. It was cheap entertainment. And that was all we cared about. Well, for me, it was mostly what I cared about.

I did not forget the ladies during this time. If anything, my preoccupation with them grew steadily throughout high school. Girls fascinated me—the way they thought, the way they talked, the way they smelled. This went way beyond the normal teen, male hormone overload. I could relate to them. They would open up and talk to me. Maybe it was the confidence of the little man all grown up or my nonchalant attitude, I don't know. But I liked it. I got a lot more satisfaction out of winning a girl's confidence than from physical involvement. As a matter of fact, I used to joke that a girl had to pretty much hit me on the head for me to realize she was attracted to me. Fortunately or unfortunately, many of them were willing to make the effort. I had several relationships, some serious, some not so serious. Out of respect, I am leaving out the details. And I would be remiss if I did not take this opportunity to ask forgiveness of any of those girls who may be reading this. I had a lot of great friends that were girls, yet there were a lot of girls that I should have been a better friend to. To the latter I am truly sorry. I could not apologize at the time because I was just too busy living hard and living from a hard heart.

TAKING ON WATER

The problem with something hard is that it can crack. I did not realize it, but the fortress I had built around my heart was not totally impenetrable. On the outside, it still looked as though I did not give a rip. My will was as strong as ever. I refused to invest myself in anything that would require an emotional attachment. My vow to not care seemed to be holding up well. Yet on the inside something was beginning to happen. I began to feel a friction building that I had not noticed before. I had basically cleared the decks in my life to make things easy and happy. So why did that happiness now seem to be draining away? Through a series of events, some small and some big, the answer became clear. Despite the fact I wanted so badly not to care, I cared anyway. The reality I tried so hard to shut out forced its way through the tiny fissures of my whitewashed walls. These events forced me to acknowledge that I was vulnerable.

Dad's wedding was definitely one of them. It was such an odd day. Part of me wanted to be there for Dad and help make sure that he was truly happy. The other part of me struggled to deal with the fact that my previous life was now officially over. In a full ceremony, Dad was marking a new beginning in his life. I knew it would be tough, but I was convinced I could get through it. I was wrong. Sure enough, I began crying softly at the back of the church when the ceremony ended. Fortunately, Dad was not around. A few other family members asked me if I was alright, and I assured them I was fine. Within a few minutes I regained my composure and rejoined the group. It may not sound like much, but to me it was unsettling. What kept me from letting this go like I did everything else? If I knew it was coming, why couldn't I keep from cracking? I struggled in vain to find an answer.

Even more questions came when I did not have time to prepare. One bright summer morning before my junior year, I got a knock at the side door. When I opened the door, I saw my buddy Nick standing there with a very strange look on his face. "Dad's dead," he said in a monotone voice. "He had a heart attack last night." I froze in disbelief. I knew it was no joke. I do not even think I said I was sorry. We got in his car and drove in complete silence to a gas station. After filling up, we drove around a while, said about two words then he dropped me back at home. The second I closed the side door behind me, overwhelming sadness gripped my entire body. I collapsed on the floor, crying uncontrollably. The pain was so intense I clutched my chest and could only utter the word "ow." I lost all control. Sure, I was sad for Nick and his family. I could not imagine a loss like that. His dad was only about 45. But there was so much more to this pain. It came on in such a rush I had no time to brace for it. Years of sadness, anger and frustration blew through what was now a gaping hole in my heart. I had never cried that hard. After what seemed like a year, I got up, wiped my face and went into the house. I was still sad, but now I was also bewildered. *"What was that about?"* I thought to myself. I did not cry nearly that hard when my own grandpa died two years earlier. I am not even sure if I cried at all. Why such a reaction now? Instead of welcoming the release of pent up emotions, I grew more and more perturbed by the unanswered questions. I swore that it would not happen again and committed to helping Nick in anyway I could.

It did not happen again, but there were still times when I cared more than I cared to. I wept with a friend who regretted her choice to terminate a pregnancy. I consoled a buddy struggling with the breakup of his own parents. And I played love doctor for lots of friends with dating issues. In each case and in several others, I fought to keep my feelings at bay while trying to maintain somewhat meaningful relationships. The joy I felt from engaging people on a deep level was now dampened by the fear of being vulnerable or losing control. This constant battle required a ton of mental and emotional energy. The easy, happy life I had invested so much in was becoming less and less easy and happy. It was actually getting to be a bummer, and it was most certainly a buzz kill. If the good times were going to keep rolling, something needed to change.

STILL HERE

I was quite a pack rat in those days. Maybe having an emotional attachment to things was easier than having one to people, or maybe I was simply too lazy to throw anything away. Either way, a lot of junk had accumulated in my room over the years. Back before we had text messaging, kids used to writes notes in school. I had baseball caps stuffed with old notes from girls dating back to middle school. In another "here's how old I am" statement, I had huge stack of 45 rpm records that had not been played in over a decade. There were unfinished drawings and half-written song lyrics stuffed everywhere. My filing system was that of having everything in a pile and every pile in its place. Around each equinox, I would get tired of the clutter or honor Mom's patient requests and finally clean up the joint.

During one of these purging sessions, something interesting happened. While riffling through one of many drawers filled with useless junk I came across a tiny lock with a key in it. I found it odd that the key was still in it and not long gone. I resisted the thought I might actually use it for something and tossed it into the trash can with several other discarded items. As I continued cleaning, my mind slowly drifted back to when I first saw that little lock. It was the night of the skating party with my cousins. I stopped cleaning instantly and sat down on my bed. The full memory of what happened that night came into view. It seemed like a thousand years ago. The memory was pleasant yet tinged with sadness. I reached down and sorted through the trash until I found the lock and key. Holding it in my hand, I reflected on the prayer and on the decision I had made. I questioned if it all really happened. Did I really ask Jesus into my heart that night? With the way I was living my life those days, it was certainly difficult to tell. As I sat and pondered the question, a warm sensation filled my body. An image formed in my mind of my heart as the lock and Jesus as the key. Peace and an assurance swept over me as my lips curled into a half smirk-half smile. Question answered. With that, I tossed the lock and key back into the drawer and moved onto something else.

A side from this wonderful vision, no great insight or deep healing came that day. But the gentle reminder stuck with me through the rest of high school. Even while continuing to seek the good life, I felt a tiny connection that I had not noticed before. I may not have been open to share my emotions, but I was at least willing to discuss my faith. I started having occasional conversations with a buddy at school who was a strong Christian. He turned me onto some big-hair-band Christian rock music, and actually got me to crack a Bible and start reading Scripture. I cannot remember where I found a Bible in our house, but I stuck with it for at least a week.

I even discussed my salvation on spring break of all things. I was in Daytona Beach with the guys, and for reasons I cannot explain, I decided to go back to the hotel by myself instead of finding another bar. On the way, a girl called out to me and invited me to sit next to her on the curb. She was attractive, so I eagerly obliged. Early in the conversation I realized this was not going to be a typical guy-girl exchange. It was obvious she was looking to witness to wayward spring breakers. Hormonally, I was disappointed, but when she asked me if I knew Jesus, I became interested on a different level. I said yes I did, even though I did not consider myself a good Christian. I am not sure she was convinced my eternity was secure, but I told her how I came to know Him, and after a few minutes of pleasant conversation, we parted company.

These seemingly random touch points gave an inkling of depth in an otherwise shallow existence. And while my desire for fun and pleasure lessened, my resistance to being open prevented the chance of giving anything much consideration. In the closing days of high school, I still knew that something needed to change. But instead of looking inward or upward for the answer, I took the easy way out and waited expectantly for college.

PART 2

The Spin Up

Chapter Five

Life Wears Thin

"Come to me, all you who are weary and burdened, and I will give you rest."

MATTHEW 11:28

GO WITH THE FLOW

Preparing for college is usually a time of great excitement, anticipation and uncertainty. Kids decide what they want to study, contemplate if they want to stay near home or go far away, and pour over financial details. For me the process was much less complex. I am not sure it could really be called a process at all. I approached college with the same apathy I had for everything else. I was absolutely, one hundred percent noncommittal. I did, however, know that I was going. My parents had always spoken of it as a foregone conclusion. I am grateful they did this because if it were left up to me, I would have never even completed my name on an application.

In the event my lack of concern seems like a joke, let me illustrate by explaining how I decided my major. In my junior year, I sat with the guidance counselor just like all my other classmates. We talked in general about my interests and about what I might like to do as a career. Since my jokes about being a brain surgeon or a fry-cook did not go over well, he gave me a list of various careers listed in alphabetical order. He instructed me to go through the list and pick something. I obliged, but my attention span was already waning, so the effort went pretty much like this: #1 Accounting. Nope, too much math; #2 Advertising. Huh, I like commercials. I could do that. Alright, Advertising it is. Done.

With the rest of my life squared away in less than thirty seconds, I asked what I needed to do next. The counselor, thoroughly frustrated by this time, gave me a list of schools offering advertising programs and a stack of applications. I picked the school that had the shortest application, which consequently was also the cheapest and easiest to get into. I ripped through the application in a scant six months, a very aggressive time frame for me back then, and by the middle of my senior year I was officially college bound.

One thing did change during this time that made the whole experience at least a little less haphazard. I changed my major to something I actually liked. I found out that the college I had chosen had a great telecommunications program. I figured I could follow my passion for music into the record industry and become a producer. I was smart enough to know that they made all the money anyway. Getting a college degree and going into production seemed a lot easier and more viable than taking the struggling musician route. And I was still all about easy.

Of course I did not realize how fortunate I was to be accepted by the one and only school I petitioned; but once it was done I was happy, if not relieved. I don't think I could have mustered the effort to fill out another application. Now, I could look forward to moving on, starting a new chapter in my life with today being the first day of the rest of that life. Blah, blah, blah. Of course I was not thinking about any of that commencement speech stuff either. All I really wanted to do was get the heck out of Dodge. I was ready for a change of scenery, and I liked the idea of being out on my own. I had never lost my desire for independence, and now came the chance to really live it. I could run free, sow my oats, and do it in an entirely different place. With all this on the horizon, it would be easy to assume I was very excited. But there was one small problem.

YAWN

I was tired. It may sound funny, but by the time I got to college, I was tired. I was "partied" out. Usually it is the time when kids are going crazy with the liberty of living on their own, and being away from the control of their parents. Instead, I arrived at college with a real "been there, done that" attitude. I was not looking to go nuts. I was just happy to start over. It seemed as if every part of me gave a collective sigh of relief. I wanted to relax and get on with my life.

I think for the first time in a while, I started to feel like I had a life. The independence I spoke of did not give me a desire to lose control; it gave me a strange sense of control. I could leave the unfortunate reality of life back home—well—back home. And that is exactly what I did, even at the expense of those closest to me. In my weariness, I could only think about what leaving meant to me, not what it meant for anybody else. The day I moved into the dorm was a perfect illustration. Mom and I loaded her little hatchback with all I owned in the world and drove the hour plus north to campus. We parked outside my dormitory and began unloading. After making several trips back and forth to the car, we stood outside the hall with nothing else to do but say goodbye. The moment I looked into her eyes, I saw a lifetime of emotions. The fullness of her perspective rushed over me like a tidal wave. She was saying goodbye to her little boy, her one and only son. More than that, she was leaving behind her roommate for the past three years and returning alone to an empty house. As her eyes filled with tears, I saw a look of pride and joy mixed with immense sadness cover her face. It was too much for me to take. I strained against the tears as we hugged. Choking on the softball that had formed in my throat, I pushed out the words "Goodbye Mom, I love you." She whispered, "Goodbye, Baby, I love you too." I wanted to say so much more, starting with thank you. I simply was not at that place. Saying those things meant accessing a lot more than I was ready to face. I felt selfish and small, and the only way out was to stuff that down along with everything else. I got the sense from Mom that she understood. She always understood.

Dad understood as well, but I know he wished I could have given more. After Thanksgiving break my freshman year, he got the chance to see exactly how tired I was. As he drove me back to campus, I realized that we were about to have another "doughnut run" talk. He explained how he and his wife were not getting along and had agreed to separate. I was ice cold. With every bit of steely calm I could muster I said, "I'm not sure what you want me to say." How is that for coldhearted? I could have made the attempt to be there for him like many times before, but this time I did not even try. My response seemed to hurt his feelings and it drove a stake into the discussion. I remember walking to my room after he dropped me off, shaking my head and shrugging off the whole talk. It might have even been better if I had said I told you so, or you made your bed, now lie in it. But again, voicing any frustration would have meant engaging my true feelings. It would have required effort. If I was going to put forth any effort at this time in my life, it was going to be for enhancing the college experience, not for facing what I had left behind.

WIDE OPEN SPACES

I quickly realized that the college experience was worthy of my focus. After all, college is a great place to live a consequence free life. And, I said I was tired, not dead. I had honed chasing the good times into a fine art, and now I had thousands of new people with which I could practice my craft. By the way, I discovered two very interesting statistics about this school shortly before I arrived. First, it was perennially rated one of the top ten party schools in the nation. Secondly, the student ratio was three to one, girls to guys. Huh, imagine the good time guy ending up in a place like that.

The sad fact is that being in this environment made it all too easy to develop several shallow relationships while generating little to no emotional output. I remember thumbing through the freshman directory with my roommate noting the names and faces of pretty girls as if it was a catalogue. We knew it would only be a matter of time until we had the chance to meet them at one of the numerous keg parties going on each weekend. By weekend, I mean Thursday, Friday and Saturday. Occasionally, Wednesday, and Sunday were added to the front and back. Really, any day was a fine opportunity for a big bash or an impromptu get together. The only hard part was those pesky eight o'clock classes the next day. And while those early classes may have been inconvenient, they did not do much to raise the difficulty level. In high school I learned the cardinal rule of breezing through classes.

Learn as quickly as you can what the teacher wants to hear and repeat that. College professors were even more obvious about what they wanted you to know, so figuring it out even with a hangover was fairly easy. My first semester I got all A's and B's. I even made the Dean's List for grade point average.

With academics securely on the back burner, I was free to get back to partying and dating. Not that I could call it dating. If I met a girl at one of the many parties, I would keep it light and make sure she did not get the wrong idea. I was definitely not looking for a long-term relationship. As a matter of fact, I had very ungracefully ended a long term relationship before I left for college. So the thought of having someone hanging around now was not exactly pegging the needle on the fun meter. Unfortunately, there were way too many girls who shared a desire for meaningless fun and as a result were willing to accept whatever I offered. I was not proud of what I did during those times, but it was all too easy to keep my heart closed off from these casual acquaintances. I found myself using romantic involvement as a kind of artificial high for my otherwise lethargic existence.

And by the end of my freshman year, I needed all the boosts I could get. Getting drunk was getting old. The incidents where my friends thought I might die from alcohol poisoning could attest to that. The eight o'clock classes were no longer an issue because I was no longer going. And my general lack of concern for anything left me lying around my room for hours on end. I put on the customary 15 or 20 pounds and my stellar debut on the Dean's List had eroded into an unimpressive array of B's C's and D's. With all this going for me, I headed back home for the summer realizing that regardless of where I was, consequences were building up in my consequence free life.

BROTHERHOOD

Dad was not impressed with my academic effort that first year. If for no other reason than he was paying my way, he had every right to be upset. However, I did get the chance to redeem myself at least a little. Dad arranged for me to work at his company in a summer intern program. It was only on the maintenance crew and it was third shift, but it offered steady work and decent pay. To be honest, the structure and real world obligation gave me exactly what I needed— a great kick in the pants. Working nights helped a lot as well. Punching in at midnight meant that I could not party throughout the week like I had been doing. I remember turning down drinks many nights knowing I had to be at work in a couple of hours.

Granted, I was not thrilled about the cramp in my social life, but it was a welcome lesson in taking responsibility. It also helped me remember that my pursuit of the social life is what had tired me out in the first place. I did not know it, but what lay ahead was a blend of social life and social responsibility that brought much needed balance to the played out, party guy.

This opportunity came from out of the blue when I got back to school for my sophomore year. Some buddies from the dorm and I agreed to get an apartment off campus. Shortly after we moved in, a couple of them said they wanted to go through rush and pledge a fraternity. I had no clue what this meant, but it sounded kind of cool, so I said I would go with them. One thing I did know was that the fraternities had the biggest and best parties. That fact alone made it worth exploring. Now, most guys rush several different fraternities and pick one if they are fortunate enough to get bids from any of them. To me that sounded like too much effort, so I only went to one. My roommate's father was member of Sigma Chi, as was his friend from high school. Since that was the extent of my exposure, I figured I would give them a try. It was a neat experience of meeting and greeting, and it gave me a chance to dust off the mature guy persona. I apparently impressed them enough to get a bid. I accepted and began the pledge process, all the while thinking, *"OK, whatever."* I could not honestly understand why I was there. It was not as if I had desire to go Greek, or a special connection to this organization. The whole process seemed so random, yet tinged with a sense of purpose. And in the same way I chose a college, it was a one shot effort. Needless to say, the importance of this decision did not reveal itself right away.

One thing that did sink in pretty quickly was the fact that fraternity life is about much more than keg parties and sorority girls. As pledges we had a lot of responsibilities placed on us. We had to keep our grades up, keep the fraternity house clean, get the active brothers up in the morning and learn the history of the organization. Unexpectedly, I found all these things meaning more to me than I thought they would. The background of Sigma Chi fascinated me. Its ideals are rooted firmly and openly in Christianity, and its symbol is a white cross. This identity gave me a subtle assurance that this was where I needed to be. And the connection to something larger than me, no matter how slight, was like a fresh breeze blowing through my stagnant world. I grew close to my pledge brothers through hard work and hours of community service. The day I was initiated as an active member was a day when I allowed myself the luxury of caring. For the first time in a long time, I actually felt proud to be a part of something.

ROCK BOTTOM

Unfortunately, the pride I felt for my accomplishment also gave me the justification to enjoy the good life once again. All this noble cause and bigger picture stuff only went so far. After I became an active brother, the obligations of pledge-ship ended, but the parties continued. In fact, they were much more enjoyable now that I did not have to work during and clean up after them. I gained the freedom to mingle with the ladies and enjoy the festivities. It started to feel like the good old days of high school, but with the added independence of living on my own. I channeled the positive energy I had received from joining a brotherhood right back into the hard-hearted party life.

Over the course of a few months, I ran through a string of brief encounters with the opposite sex, rekindled an old relationship that was now completely inappropriate, and added marijuana and gambling to my party activities. I did all this because I didn't care. I know I said I didn't care in high school, but now I seemed to not care with a vengeance. For no specific reason, I eagerly went off the deep end. I doubt any one could tell on the outside, because my façade seldom flinched. But on the inside, I was so cold you could store meat on my heart. If I stole a buddy's girlfriend, it was too bad for that guy. I showed up to class drunk? So what, who hadn't? Lied to a girl just to avoid seeing her again? That was standard protocol.

If there was an end in sight, I could not see it. As the semester drew to a close, I packed up my dad's truck and left my apartment vacant for the summer—vacant because I was too lazy to find someone to sublet. No big deal, right? With that concern cast off like all the others, I drove home with every intention of continuing the good times.

What happened that summer was far from good times. I got arrested, again, for underage consumption, this time with a fake ID. My inappropriate relationship came to a deeply sinful conclusion, and my gambling got out of hand. Basically, my entire life had gotten out of hand. This realization slapped me in the face on two separate occasions that summer. The first was during a night of heavy drinking and gambling at a friend's house. We kept gambling into the wee hours primarily because I was losing and wouldn't quit until I got even. Finally, at about $1,500 down, I got mad and told my friend I was going to pay up. We jumped in my car and I started driving like mad toward the bank where I was going to empty my account. My friend urged me to turn around and said I did not have to pay. Ignoring him, I sped on, swerving wildly. As I peeled around the corner to the road leading into town, the thought finally crashed into my drunken head: *"What the hell are you doing?! Is this really worth killing yourself?"* In a fit of wisdom that was far beyond me, I turned to my buddy and said, "I can't do this." The phrase referred to so much more than operating a vehicle. Something within me broke at that moment. I turned the car around and some how made it back to the house without killing us both.

Not long after that night, I had the chance to party back on campus before the school year started. I drove up to school by myself and hunted around for the party. I stopped in at a few placed I knew and felt more and more foolish each time I did not find my friends. Eventually I gave up looking and sat silently in my car wondering what to do. Suddenly I remembered the phrase I had uttered not two weeks before and my heart sank. I felt the energy drain from my body. I was totally dejected and disgusted with myself. Without the energy to drive home, I wandered over to my vacant apartment and opened the door. It was empty and dark, a perfect match for my heart at that time. I shut the door behind me and slid down against the wall. The loneliness and isolation of the choices I had made washed over me as I slumped over and lay on the bare floor. I did not even have the strength to cry. With nothing else to do, I slowly drifted off to sleep with one thought repeating in my mind. *"This was quite a life I had carved out for myself."*

RAYS OF HOPE

At some point during the night in that empty apartment, I made a decision. Not a scream from the rooftop, etched in stone decision—more of a subconscious choice. I was simply done being that guy. My tiredness had become full-blown exhaustion. I gave up trying to shrug off the ramifications of my actions. I admitted I was hurting people indiscriminately and it sickened me. I realized that thinking only of me, or not really thinking at all, was not the ticket to the good life. I knew that at best it was an express pass to a shallow, meaningless existence, and at worst it was a slippery slope to an early grave. Even though I was dead tired, the grave was not a pleasant thought. And though I once reveled in what was shallow and meaningless, I began losing my taste for that as well. It was time to move on. It was time to grow up—high time.

As I drove home from campus the following day, my mind sifted through the events of the past few months looking for anything positive on which I could build. I soon settled on a memory of Mom and me in the church she had recently started attending. It seemed odd that I would be anywhere near church during this time in my life, but Mom had been graciously inviting me, so I occasionally obliged her. On one particular Sunday, I remembered the words of the sermon shooting like a laser beam to my heart. I was convicted of how I had been living my life and of the hurt I had caused. When the pastor gave an altar call, I was instantly compelled. I whispered to Mom, "I have to go up," and I was halfway down the isle before I realized what I was doing. I knelt on the steps and began praying for God to forgive me. I prayed in earnest for him to forgive my sins, as I knew I was committing some of the biggies. I cannot say I felt any significant cleansing at the time, but I was truly repentant. As I reflected on it now in the car, I realized how much I had kept on sinning. As the desire for forgiveness welled up again, I said simply, "Lord, please forgive me." I figured that was all that needed to be said, and it was more than I had said to Him in years.

The prayer faded into the background as I remembered another bright spot from the previous semester. I met a girl. Yes, I know, I met a lot of girls, but this one was different—much different. She sat behind me in Anthropology class. A fraternity brother in the same class told me her name was Angela. About the only thing I remember from the class was that she would give me the sweetest smile and say hi every time she walked by my desk. She seemed so nice and popular; I knew she had to be dating someone. I am thankful I did not get up the nerve to ask her out myself. With the state I was in at the time, I had no ability to treat a girl like that the way she should be treated. But as I smiled and thought about her now, I wondered if I would get the chance to meet her again.

From that day on, I quit the gambling and the weed. Gambling I was not good at and smoking grass just made me feel so stupid. I seriously curtailed my drinking and I lost all desire to get drunk. I finished out the summer working landscape and saving whatever money I could. I signed on to live in the fraternity house my junior year, and as the fall semester approached, I looked forward to it with a sense of optimism that I had never felt before.

Chapter Six

Two Ladies, One Lifeline

"Then you will look and be radiant, your heart will throb and swell with joy; the wealth on the seas will be brought to you, to you the riches of the nations will come."

ISAIAH 60:5

FRESH START

There was nothing particularly significant to be optimistic about, but as I coasted into my junior year things felt clean and new. I got the deep sense that a great opportunity, a second chance, awaited me. Along with this sense, I felt something I had not experienced in a long time: desire. Not the desire for pleasure and good times that I had before, or a desire to be independent; this was a desire to do things right. I genuinely wanted to show more care and concern for the people and things in my life. The problem was that I did not really know how to do that. I had gone so long without feeling anything or choking down what I did feel, I doubted I could act any other way. This created an odd sense of balance in me. While I was no longer angrily opposed to caring, I was not exactly gushing with emotions either. As the year started, I settled into an ambivalent, wait-and-see attitude.

On the surface, I had all the typical new school year things to keep me excited. I moved into the fraternity house with most of my pledge brothers. We had a great time catching up and pitching in to get the house ready to go for the first party of the year. I know I said my desire for the good times had waned, but I could not resist the energy of the first weekend. As our party ramped up that Saturday night, I rose to the occasion. I danced and sang, and hugged and chugged right alongside the throngs of kids that were jammed into our basement. I saw what seemed like hundreds of old friends and I made a lot of new friends too. For some reason, I felt like I owned the place. I do not know if it was my new balanced attitude or the fact that I had no agenda whatsoever, but the ladies seemed to take notice. I am in no way bragging, but I had more girls ask me out that one night than had asked in my previous 20 years combined. I could hardly believe it. It was fortunate I had chosen not to drink much. Otherwise, I would not have had the forethought to get anyone's phone number.

As the night wore down, I forgot about all of those numbers anyway, because in walked the girl from my Anthropology class. She was more beautiful than I had remembered. Right when I thought my night could not get any better, it instantly became one of the greatest nights of my life. I think we danced a little, but we mostly talked. We asked each other how the summer went and discussed our class schedules. I am glad we didn't talk about anything too deep because I kept getting lost in her smile. It was absolutely captivating and matched only by the brightness in her eyes. We leaned against the wall outside my room for a few minutes, but it seemed like forever. I probably would have stood there forever, but in a miraculous moment of inspiration, I asked if I could call her sometime. She said yes, so I scrambled into my room, grabbed a slip of paper and jotted down her number. She left a little while later and I have no clue what I did after that.

First Date

To this day I defend my stance that she was the only girl I actually called from that night. And now it's in print, so that should count for something. Granted, it took me two weeks to get around to calling her, but she was the only one. I honestly do not know why I waited so long to call her. Nerves were definitely part of the equation. I could not shake the fact that she seemed too sweet and attractive to not already be in a relationship. I also played the game of "don't call her too quickly" in my mind. Yet I think the main reason I hesitated stemmed from the fact that this was uncharted territory for me. The feelings I had for Angela went way beyond infatuation, way beyond physical attraction. From the small amount of time we had spent together, I knew she was someone I wanted to have in my life. Before I called her that was all I knew. Something inside me kept me from stressing about what could be. I decided to stay relaxed and see where things would lead.

We picked up the conversation right where we left off when I finally did call her. We both agreed pretty quickly that a date was the next order of business, but as we looked at our schedules, we realized it was going to be tough to make it happen. Rush had started for fraternities and sororities, and we each had something to do every night of the week, including the weekend. As a compromise, we decided that an early dinner on Wednesday would be the best chance to get together. I suppose we could have waited until after rush, but given my delinquency in calling her, I am fortunate she was willing to go at all. So even if it did not sound all that romantic, I committed to pick her up early on Wednesday.

It may not have been romantic, but it was amazing—amazing and effortless. I was not nervous. I had no expectations. I definitely had no secret agenda. I only looked forward to finding out more about this stunning lady. I made sure to pick her up on time, and from there we drove to a nice seafood restaurant chain. It may not have been a five star meal, but on a college budget, anything not handed out from a drive through window is considered fine dining. We really did not care about the food anyway. If I was concerned, I would have ordered something much more graceful than crab legs.

But with crab shell pieces flying and butter dripping, we engaged in one of the greatest conversations I have ever had. It was my first real conversation with a girl in years. We talked as if we had always known each other, except for the added excitement of everything being new. Nothing was off limits. We talked about family, friends, faith and many other things that did not start with the letter "f". I could not believe how much I opened up, or how comfortable I felt doing it. Not only did I want to know her, I wanted her to know me. I was not even sure I knew me at that time in my life, but I could not hold anything back from her. She was so warm and honest. Passion and energy lit up her eyes. Combined with that bright smile and beautiful blond hair, they created a picture of loveliness that made it hard to concentrate.

We easily could have talked until they threw us out of the restaurant, but we both had rush events to attend. So reluctantly we finished up and I drove her home. Still regretting that the night had to end, I pulled to the curb in front of her house and stopped. Instead of offering to walk her to the door, I simply said, "I had a great time." She said the same, and without so much as an awkward pause, she hopped out of the car and went into the house. That was it. No kiss. No hug. I did not even shake her hand! What was I thinking? I did manage to sneak in an "I'll call you." But aside from that, the greatest date of my life ended just that quickly. I drove back to the house on a high from the evening and with two things on my mind. One, I knew that something big had taken place. And two, I knew I was not going to wait another two weeks to call this girl.

HOMECOMING

OK, don't blow it. As the days passed, that thought kept circling around my mind. Angela and I continued in our busy schedules, but we did manage to talk on the phone a couple of times. After each conversation, the sense grew stronger and stronger that this fledgling relationship was meant to be. Everything felt so right I wanted nothing to go wrong. I had treated so many girls badly before, I did not want to do that to Angela. I knew I should take things slowly, but not too slowly. The more I found myself starting to care for her, the more I yearned for things to be perfect. And yet, in the midst of this seemingly high pressure situation, I realized something. Things were perfect. Not because I was trying to make them so, because I was letting them be. I was open and honest, both with myself and with her. I did not try to fake any emotions, and I did not try to hold back any feelings. As for where this was going, I knew I was not in control, and that thought actually gave me comfort.

Another thing I could not control was our social calendars. Things are very busy in the life of a fraternity or sorority member, with all the parties and mixers and formal dances. All that socializing can really hamper one's social life. It would have been very tough for Angela and I to find more time to see each other if it was not for one simple fact. Her sorority and my fraternity were paired together for homecoming. For those who may not know, homecoming refers to the first home football game of the year in high school and college. It is usually a big event, but at a party school like ours, it was a multi-day extravaganza. With an event lined up for every night of the week, this meant we would be fulfilling our social obligations while spending quality time together. It was an ideal situation. It was perfection.

It felt as though the whole week was planned just for her and me. Each night, Angela and her sorority sisters would show up at our house in force. We would go through the obligatory games and meet-and-greet sessions. Then as soon as we could, Angela and I would sneak off to some place quieter so we could talk. And boy, did we talk! I never talked that much with a girl in my life. But in the same manner as our first date, the conversation flowed naturally. It would not have been any more easy and open than if I were talk talking to my best friend. And that is really how I began to see her. Well, that is not the only way I began to see her.

I would be lying if I said my romantic attraction to Angela wasn't also growing with each meeting that week. Every time I saw her, she appeared to be more beautiful than the last. As she revealed more and more about her self, I was able to peer into a richness and depth of character that was completely enchanting. This one-two punch of inward and outward beauty was enough to knock me for a loop. Of course my fraternity brothers quickly realized what was going on and ribbed me mercilessly. Angela's sorority sisters also joined in the fun at our expense, but neither one of us paid any attention. We both acknowledged that week that something monumental was taking shape. We agreed to take it slowly and let the guiding force we both felt lead the way.

MOM 2.0

This guiding force in my life now had a lot more prevalence thanks to another very special lady. Remember I said that Mom had started attending church again? Well, she had actually started a lot more than that. She had begun a new life.

I did not notice a big change in her at first; mostly because I did not notice much of anything in the years following the divorce. But as one would expect, Mom had a tough time trying to get on with living after her marriage ended. She tried to get out and have fun. She even engaged in a couple of dating relationships. Yet from my point of view, it seemed like everything in her life was tinged with sadness. Again, no one could blame her if that was truly the case. But in all honesty, it was hard to tell. The difficulty stemmed from the fact that she showed so little emotion. If she was sad, she got over it. If she was mad, she might blow up briefly, but it would quickly pass. In any case, she had a very rational view that, while feelings were important, they should not be allowed to control one's life. I appreciated this, and appreciated that I was raised in a very rational, loving, nurturing environment.

As I went off to college, I knew that Mom was sad, but I also had a sense that she was ready for a change. She moved out of the house we lived in and into a nice, small place of her own. Her sisters attended a small Baptist church in town, and she began joining them on Sundays and Wednesdays. In the midst of all this, she must have found what had been missing, because it was clear, even to me, that she rededicated her life to Jesus Christ. That is when I noticed the change.

When I came home from college on the weekends, I now noticed a still, small voice in my ear. It sounded a lot like Mom's voice. Actually, it was Mom's voice. As I mentioned, she began patiently and lovingly inviting me to join her for services. At first I resisted and made the usual excuses. I cannot say I was worried about getting struck by lightening, but maybe I should have been. Eventually, I agreed to go out of respect for her. It was during this time that I had my "compulsion to repent" experience. That event coupled with Mom's persistence led me to start attending each weekend I was home and over the summer months. Slowly I began to view church as an "I know I should go" kind of thing.

Throughout this period, I continued to see a change in Mom. She had always displayed a warm heart, and now that warm heart looked to be softening even more. There was a gentleness, peace and calm about her nature that I had never seen. Even in her persistence with my church attendance, there was a graciousness that went way beyond a Mom trying to get her son to live righteously. She never condemned, never cajoled and never, ever used an ounce of guilt. For that I was truly grateful. This was the first time in my life I had seen someone's love for the Lord flow through them transparently. Though I would not admit it at the time, Mom's witness was more compelling than a month of Sundays. On a level I could not articulate, I felt an assurance that Mom was truly experiencing a transformation. With this came a subtle hope for my own future, and a strong peace that Mom was going to be all right.

SEISMIC SHIFT

How does the heart of one man stand up against the powerful onslaught of care and compassion from two such amazing ladies? The answer is it doesn't. My heart never stood a chance. All the efforts to close myself off and live a life without connecting to anything or anybody were adding up to a miserable failure. I was losing this battle. The fortress I had built to hold my feelings captive was being dismantled brick by brick before my very eyes. In my fatigue, I let my guard down for a brief moment, and my opponent gained the advantage. I was attacked at my most vulnerable point by two unassuming daughters of Christ. And knowing they had Him on their side, I raised the white flag without so much as a single shot in retaliation.

OK, enough of the war analogy. I did not really feel this way at all. I did not feel defeated, or destroyed, deceived or deprived. I did not feel as though I had lost anything. On the contrary, I felt liberated and rejuvenated. It was as if a whole new world had opened up before me. In this world I could care for someone and allow someone to care for me. Not because it looked like the right thing do, but because I genuinely wanted to do it. I could not only solicit someone else's emotions, I could also share mine openly without fear of where it might lead. I was no longer worried about being hurt, and I definitely had a desire to not hurt others. In a relatively brief span, I went from refusing to care to not caring that I cared.

The span of time in which this change occurred was not nearly as surprising as the ease with which it happened. There was no struggle, no recoil, and no red flag. In situations before, a bell would go off in my head notifying me that things were getting too deep. I would tell myself, *It is not worth it. Time to move on.* It was as if I had a miniature Robbie the Robot inside my brain yelling, *Danger, danger!* In the case with Angela, I do not even recall having that internal conversation. I think it took me about a half a second to weigh the risks against the rewards before making the choice to pursue a real relationship with her. If there was any significant risk, it stemmed from what I would lose if I did not have this girl in my life.

My relationship with Mom, though not as new and exciting for obvious reasons, also had a dramatic effect on me. I watched a long dormant dimension of my life come alive through her faithful obedience and devotion. In short, I was beginning to acknowledge my spirit. This was a big step for a child raised in a home where church had no relevance, and a young adult who tried desperately to live only from the mind.

During the final years of college, a hazy, distant, almost surreal image formed deep within me. I pictured myself in a tiny life boat on a huge body of water, drifting from the shallows to the deep. In my mind this image should have caused panic. In my heart it would have triggered an immediate shut down. But on my spirit, there was an overriding peace. This peace provided the understanding that deep relationships were the true source of happiness. According to the image, I was definitely now in uncharted waters. In reality I knew it meant that an enormous shift had taken place. And in both settings, instead of straining against what was happening, I decided to embrace the change.

The Guiding Hand

As if one could not see it coming, all of this change in my mind, heart and spirit was leading to one inevitable destination: love. Yes, I said it—the big "L" word. I had to admit I was falling in love with Angela. Everything about our relationship felt so right, I think we both knew it long before we said it out loud. Shortly after homecoming we agreed to date each other exclusively. I met her family and instantly felt accepted. We continued to talk about everything, and occasionally we would even skip a party to be alone and talk well into the night. As our feelings grew, our conversations began to focus more and more on the future. If we talked about kids, we talked about how to raise them together. If we talked about jobs, we discussed cities where we could both find work. It all seemed to flow without question or doubt. There was even a time where Angela caught herself talking about "our kids" instead of kids in general. Of course I could not let her live down that slip of the tongue, but she was only speaking the way be both felt. Although we couldn't see or predict the future, what we knew lay ahead was our future. On a level we could barely describe, we had been knitted together, and we looked on with patient expectation as things unfolded.

Mom, in her wisdom, had a good idea of where things were going. She had grown fond of Angela over the months, and I know she wanted us to be sure that our relationship had a solid foundation. One night while staying at her house, I came home to find a note on my pillow along with a plan of salvation pamphlet. The note simply asked if I knew my Savior. I smiled and thanked God for Mom's care and concern. I reflected on the decision I had made so long ago. My heart was warmed by the times He had reminded me of it, and I marveled at how close and real that choice still felt. In fact, it was more real to me now than it ever had been. I assured Mom of this the following morning, and I went on to explain how Angela had asked the Lord into her heart at the same age. We uncovered this during one of our many conversations, and to us it was yet another sign of how the Lord had brought us together. Mom was comforted by my words, and I felt deeply blessed to know that she was praying for us.

Angela and I were now openly expressing our love for each other, and in some ways I still could not believe how far I had come in such a short time. I laughed out loud when I thought about the day that I vowed never to love or be loved. I shrugged off the statement because now it sounded so ridiculous. It did not even feel like I was the one who said it. I had the image in my mind of an old, cheesy B movie or a sappy daytime soap opera. I saw myself as the bad leading actor saying those words and playing to the camera for melodramatic effect. I thanked God that I no longer felt that way, and I thanked Him for taking the time to show me what true love could be.

Chapter Seven

A Real-life Love Story

"May your fountain be blessed, and may you rejoice in the wife of your youth...may you ever be captivated by her love."

PROVERBS 5:18-19

WHAT LOVE IS

True love, as I was beginning to discover, is unconditional. This may not be earth shattering news to anyone, but to me it was a front page story. In fact, everything about love at this point in my life was critical information. After years of taking it for granted, pushing it away, and vowing never to feel it, I had to re-learn love from the ground up. I needed to get more comfortable sharing my feelings. I had to figure out how to openly show my emotions in a positive way. Basically, I had to do all the things that guys hate to do. And I needed to do them well. After all, when God brings you someone you are supposed to spend the rest of your life with, it is probably a good idea to honor that gift with your best effort.

I got that message loud and clear as I saw my relationship with Angela blow past the expectations either of us had. We could not believe how amazing and exciting it was. And not just at the start. Sure, we had the usual lovey-dovey phase. I would bring her a rose or a gift every time I saw her. She would stare longingly into my eyes. We would make our friends sick whenever we were together. But as time wore on, we both realized that the relationship was not picking up any friction. We were not getting on each other's nerves. We did not grow tired of being together or get restless if we had nothing to do. As the initial infatuation faded, we found something in its place: unconditional love.

Neither of us would have termed it that way, but that is what we had. I knew no matter what happened, nothing could make me stop loving Angela. And I knew that no matter what I did, she would never stop loving me. This assurance gave us the freedom not to take each other for granted but to put each other first. I genuinely cared about Angela's happiness more than my own. Not out of obligation but out of admiration. Mutual respect drove me to first consider her desires and feelings. If it was important to her, I wanted to know so that it could become important to me. I found myself truly putting forth my best effort, but I also found that the more I gave the more I received. What that did was make the effort effortless. I did not strive to make things perfect and neither did Angela. We caught on very early that the less we tried to force happiness, the more happiness came to us. We learned that the best thing we could do for the relationship was to let it be. If we had somewhere to go that was great. If we did not, that was great as well. If our plans got messed up, no big deal, we were still together. Some of our most entertaining dates happened when we had no plans at all. The bottom line was that it did not matter what we did as a couple. It mattered who we were as a couple. We invested ourselves into being the best we could be for each other. And that seemed to make a huge difference.

The difference was so big; in fact, most of our friends took notice. They would say things like: "You guys have such a great relationship." or "You two are so good together." We tried not to sound prideful when we agreed, but we had to acknowledge it. We would have loved to explain that it was a God thing, but not many kids in college were open to hearing that. Maybe we should have been bolder, because what we did notice was that a relationship like ours was very rare. And again, not wanting to sound prideful, but we did not see anyone else that had what we had. This made both of us sad, but also extremely thankful. And it made us cherish what God had provided all the more.

POP GOES THE QUESTION

I walked out to the dock at daybreak and stood in the peace of a perfect Wisconsin summer morning. As I gazed at the reflections in the glassy, calm water, I contemplated the step I was about to take. I laughed quietly when I looked back at how far I had come. The foolish child who vowed never to love anyone was now a young man about to ask the most amazing lady for her hand in marriage. I was thankful. I was happy. I was tired.

I had stayed up all night playing cards with Angela's cousins at the family cottage. Since most of her family had gathered there for a vacation, I seized it as the perfect time and setting to pop the question. Today was the day, and it would have been nice to get some sleep. But I shrugged it off knowing that I was too excited to sleep anyway. I had been planning this for weeks. I smuggled the ring to the cottage in my suitcase. I wrote a poem just for the event. I wanted to ask her father first out of respect, and then take a rowboat out to the middle of the lake and ask her there. She was so special and what we had was so special, I wanted this day to be special as well. It was a storybook day for the most part.

Morning gave way to a hot afternoon, and the whole family had gathered outside to enjoy the sun and water. As time wore on, I started getting a little anxious waiting for the chance to talk to Angela's dad without everyone else around. Finally, in what had to be divine intervention, he started washing cars by the side of the cabin. I quickly grabbed a rag and joined him. When I felt sure that no one else was coming, I began my speech. I barely got the words permission and daughter's hand out of my mouth by the time he threw down the rag and lifted me off the ground with a huge bear hug. I assumed this meant he approved, so I moved down to the dock where Angela was sunbathing to suggest a boat ride. She said no.

At this point her dad was already pacing and I knew there was no going back. I chose to say something like: "Aw, come on, it'll be fun." instead of, "Just get in the boat." Thankfully, she relented and I rowed us out near the center of the small lake. Now safely away from the crowd on the beach, I took the poem from my pocket and read it out loud to her. Since I had written her poems before, she did not catch on to what was happening. She thanked me for the beautiful words and gave me a kiss. Then I got on my knees. A confused look settled on her face as the boat rocked and I fumbled through my pocket for the much smaller ring. As I held it up, I asked if she would marry me. Her countenance instantly changed to excitement and disbelief as she said yes and plunged into my arms. The boat rocked wildly and I stared at the ring thinking, *Maybe this was a bad idea.* Fortunately the boat settled as we sat back down. I slipped the ring on Angela's finger very quickly, and we rowed for what seemed like hours back to shore. By this time, Angela's dad was wearing tracks in the grass. As we approached, several of the ladies realized what had happened and erupted with screams of joy. After several minutes of laughter, tears and numerous pats on the back, I found my way to our tent for a much needed rest. In the thirty seconds it took me to fall asleep, I marveled at how predestined this all felt. I was now more certain than ever that Angela and I were made for each other. Our lives together had blown away any concept of what I thought was possible. And the love and joy I experienced that day convinced me that so much more was yet to come.

Hearts Grow Fonder

Angela and I were both excited by what the future held in store for us. Yet we also knew that rushing into a marriage was not the best way to make that future all it could be. Being patient and relaxed had brought us so many blessings to this point; we saw no reason to change that now. Besides, there was no way to logistically coordinate the hundreds of relatives on Angela's side of the family in a short span of time. No, this was going to be a long engagement. We set the date for September of the following year, and accepted the reality of a long-distance relationship.

There was never a question that the relationship could bear the strain of living apart. In addition to all the other great qualities it had, our love also contained a great deal of maturity. Angela and I discovered a wonderful balance between our devotion to each other and the need to remain individuals. We chose to embrace the opportunity to live alone and establish our careers, as well as our independence. For me it was nothing new. Inside I had been living alone for years. But now, with a newfound hope for the future and a budding faith, I pulled from the positive aspects of self-sufficiency to prepare for this time. For Angela, it was a little different. Though she had never lived alone, either physically or figuratively, she was raised with an independent spirit. After graduating with a degree in social work, she took a new job in a new city. She decided to get an apartment by herself despite the uncertainty of having no one around for the first time in her life. I admired her courage and also her commitment to a career she loved.

The two years we lived apart were great for both of us, but I am not going to lie and say it was all a bowl of cherries. I admit, being away from her stunk. Simply put, I missed my best friend. Angela was closer to me than anyone ever had been. I told her things that I would not tell anyone else. Her warmth and compassion drew me out of my hardened shell. She listened lovingly and gracefully as I shared the darkness of my past. I kept nothing back from her and she never flinched. She never judged, never seemed shocked or offended. I could tell that she only wanted to understand and be there for me. And I wanted her to know the same about me. When she shared things from her past she was not proud of, I endured the sadness and regret with her. But at the same time, I felt honored and privileged to be invited into her world. She could have told me anything, and it would have served only to deepen my care and concern for her.

This openness and comfort had been cemented in our daily contact while at school. Now we yearned for the chance to see each other every day, even if it was only for a few minutes. At school, if something happened, she could be the first person I told. She could also be the last person I spoke to before kissing her goodnight and walking back to the fraternity house. Living apart, we resorted to talking on the phone a couple times a week and maybe seeing each other on the weekends. We made the most of those weekends with long walks and quiet dinners. But Sunday night would come all too quickly and I would soon be heading home. I felt like punching whoever started the saying: "Absence makes the heart grow fonder." Especially during the winters where I would risk life and limb driving three hours on the icy northern Indiana roads. My only solace was that I knew this was temporary. Eventually, the wedding day would come and we could finally be together.

TOGETHER AS ONE

It was another perfect morning. This one surpassed even that day at the lake. It was warm but not humid. One could tell it was early fall by the slight crispness in the air. A few light clouds gave such a vivid contrast to the deep blue sky it looked as though someone had painted the whole thing. Standing outside the hotel, I drank in the warmth of the sun's rays. I took a deep breath and let it out, feeling glad for the chance to be by myself before the hustle and bustle of the day began. I then headed across the street to get a quick bite of breakfast. As I made the brief walk, I found myself once more contemplating my situation. Yet this time I was not reflecting on how far I had come, I was looking expectantly to the future; not in a hurry-up-and-see-how-it-turns-out sort of way, but with a genuine excitement and desire to begin the adventure. I was ready to start a life with this beautiful woman, and I knew that no matter what lay ahead we would see it together.

On the journey back to the room, a sense of calm and contentment washed over me. My thoughts drifted back to the task at hand. The future would come, but the wedding had to happen first. We waited a long time for this day, and now that it was finally here, I felt great anticipation but no anxiety. I was convinced that this day was going to be like everything else in our relationship—effortless. I know that a lot of weddings are stressful. Ours was not. We didn't have a big budget, so pomp and circumstance were the first things to go. We focused all of our effort and resources on having a good time. And that is exactly what we did. Everyone did.

I remembered someone saying that the day goes by so fast it is hard to enjoy it. I wanted to slow everything down so I could really enjoy it. I wanted to live in the fullness of the moment and remember all the details. One detail I could never forget was seeing Angela for the first time as she walked down the isle. I hope every groom can say this about his bride: she made me absolutely breathless. At that moment, the fullness of her beauty overwhelmed me. Her hair, makeup and dress were flawless, but they paled in comparison to the light in her eyes and the radiance of her smile. Tears filled my eyes as I was struck by the realization that she was coming to be united with me. I felt humbled, honored, blessed, proud, and elated, along with about fifty other emotions. But, they all took a back seat to love at that moment. I could not believe that anyone could feel this much love for another person. I was truly captivated.

Before I could stop myself, I uttered the only word that came to mind. "Wow." It may not have been profound, but at least I didn't yell it at the top of my lungs. I managed to regain composure and hold it together long enough to make it through the ceremony. Except for a few minor glitches everything went perfect. I did put her ring on the wrong finger, and I forgot to kiss her at the end, but instead of stressing about it, we laughed about it. Besides, I was pretty sure the whole thing still counted.

OUT OF THE GATE

A great day ended with a great reception. It was the kind of party that people talk about for years. Of course Angela and I were busy meeting and greeting and thanking people, but we could see everyone was having a really good time. The next day we had to ask ourselves questions like: "Did I really see your great-aunts dancing with my fraternity brothers?" Knowing the answers, we simply laughed and shook our heads as we loaded up the car for our honeymoon trip. We were ready for our first big adventure as husband and wife.

The car was not a limo waiting to whisk us away for a week on some tropical island. No, it was Angela's old Volkswagen loaded down with bikes and luggage for a trek to the mountains. We decided to drive from Indiana to Colorado and spend a week hiking and biking in the Rockies. To us it sounded a lot more enjoyable than lying on a beach all day. And, for the most part, it was very enjoyable. The only issue came when the car started having problems on the drive out there. We got trapped in rush hour traffic in Denver with a car that wanted to die every time it went up a hill. This was a tough problem to have heading into the Rocky Mountains. As we struggled to stay clear of several semis and faster cars, Angela and I both decided to pray. Fearing for our lives, we prayed together like never before. We asked for God's protection the rest of the way. By His grace, two hours later, we pulled into the bed and breakfast where we were staying and nearly kissed the ground when we got out of the car.

It may not have seemed like that much of a trial, but to us it was significant. It was the first time we had gone to God as a couple in a serious time of need. To this point, we were thankful for what He had given us, but we had never called out for Him to protect us. For me personally, it was a big wake-up call that I now had more than myself to worry about. I started to understand that loving Angela went a lot deeper than merely caring about her. I had to care for her as well. As her husband, I was responsible for her physical, emotional and spiritual well being. Granted, she could still take care of herself, but I wanted to step up and be the man she needed me to be. During that treacherous drive, I felt the weight of my new role, and I welcomed it. It fit well. Like a suit of armor, it felt noble and honorable. I experienced a deeper meaning and purpose to my life. A feeling of pride welled up inside me. Though I sensed its sizeable heft, the pressure on my spirit was not laborious. It was joyous. I was grateful for this role and all its responsibilities.

As far as mishaps go, the rest of the trip, at least, was uneventful. We had an unbelievable time exploring the mountain trails on foot and on the bikes. We made the trip home in one piece and prepared to start our lives together. Home for us was now Cincinnati, Ohio. Only a few weeks earlier it was going to be Columbus, Ohio, but a sudden job transfer had me pulling up stakes right before the wedding. No worries. We rolled with the tide and found an apartment a few minutes from my office. Angela transferred from her job in Indiana, and we both went back to work. We were excited to see what it really felt like to live together.

DAY BY DAY

It is often said that the first year of marriage is the toughest. If that was true, Angela and I were in for a very cushy life. Our first year was just as much of a storybook as everything else in our relationship to that point. I think the biggest reason was because we did not try to make it a storybook. We didn't try to make it anything. I am sure Angela had a picture of marriage in her mind as a young girl. I think every little girl dreams about the white picket fence life, but those innocent dreams did not make their way into our relationship as some secret agenda. Based on the numerous other relationships we had seen that suffered from this, I was extremely thankful that she was too emotionally stable to let that happen.

As for me, I was amazed that I had made it this far. I felt like I had won the lottery. I had no dreams of what my marriage would be like because I could not even fathom myself being married. Since this was all brand new to me, I knew I needed to go with the flow. Whether it was her maturity or my ignorance having a hand in it or not, we had no rigid plan of what married life should be like. If anything, we had some idea of what it should not be like. She had seen her parents go through tough times and I have covered what happened to mine. So we knew that we did not want to cause each other pain. Yet at the same time, we knew we could not live in fear of something happening.

This is where I know our faith played a big part. I wish I could say that it was a total faith in God, but at this point in our lives we were not quite there. Yes, we acknowledged Him, we thanked Him, and we even prayed to Him for protection. But in this first year, we looked at it more as having faith in our love. We knew that what we had was a lot bigger than the two of us. So when we had disagreements—and yes, we did have them—there was an overriding desire to respect each other and preserve the marriage. When we did fight, we fought about the usual dumb things: my toothpaste was cold, or I left the cap off my feet. Wait. Well, you know what I mean. The point is it was all pointless. No argument was worth hurting each other's feelings. We strived to not let the sun go down on our anger. And we always enjoyed making up.

If we had any serious conflict, it was most often because one of us was focused too much on trying to please the other. A perfect case in point is where I would try to fix a problem she was having when all she wanted was for me to listen. I had a tough time in that department. I did not want anything to be wrong in her life, so I was Mr. Fix-it. If I interrupted her venting process, she would get frustrated and start crying. This I could not handle. I came from a family where I saw tears about as often as snowballs in July, so crying for "no reason" did not make sense to me. But I cared for her, and I slowly started to understand that solving a problem did not always make things better. With this in mind, I trained myself to remember the "don't try so hard" rule. It actually made it easier, because instead working on things, I was now free to simply love her. And that was something I knew I could do right.

Chapter Eight

Thawing Out

And so we know and rely on the love God has for us. God is love.
Whoever lives in love lives in God, and God in him."

John 4:16

Good Life

As Angela and I settled into our lives, we began to take advantage of all that surrounded us. Since both of us worked, we had more than enough money to pay the bills, put some away and have fun. Being young and without children, the having fun part quickly filtered to the top our list. And there was no shortage of fun things to do in our new town. I had several friends from work that were all our age and loved to have a good time. We would frequently start those good times right at five o'clock in the local watering hole. If we wanted to take in the weekend night life, we would head downtown and catch some live music from a band we knew. If the band was not playing, any place that had a dance floor was all right with Angela. To stay in shape, we worked out together and went hiking in the hills whenever we could get away. We also took the opportunity to really get out of town; two weeks in Europe, a week in Napa Valley, several trips out of state to visit friends. We definitely made use of our vacation time and our free time.

But the thing that made all this really great was that we never had to be doing something. There was no pressure to always be on the go or always be partying. I never felt like saying, "I need to cut loose," or "we've got to get away." And Angela didn't say things like: "You never take me out." We had plenty to do and if we did it, that was awesome. Yet we were also happy to sit around the house on a Friday night like an old married couple. We could sit on the couch reading or watching TV. We could go for a relaxing stroll while holding hands and talking. Yes, talking. Believe it or not, we had not run out of things to say to each other. If something happened, I still wanted her to be the first person I told. And I still wanted to hear all about her day as well. This made it all the more enjoyable to be together without needing a distraction. In the same manner that we tried to avoid making our marriage anything, we allowed our social life to follow suit. For us it was not about being busy, it was about being together.

While our time was focused on quality, our finances continued to take care of the quantity. As a social worker, Angela was not exactly rolling in the dough, but her income did help. Mine was another story. I had worked my way into an Information Technology job just in time to take advantage of the Internet boom. I was increasing my income by thirty percent or better each year, and we were increasing our lifestyle as well. Angela and I both liked shiny things. If one could wear it, it was on her list. If one could drive it, it was on mine. This created an odd dynamic, because Angela came from a family that had struggled financially. So even though she liked nice things, she had a hard time justifying any purchase. The price of a pair of shoes could make her queasy. I, on the other hand, had no real concern for money. If I wanted something, I bought it. This frustrated Angela when we would shop together. Every time she would comment that something was nice, my response was "buy it." Now this was partly because shopping was not my favorite pastime, but it was also because I wanted her to have nice things. To me, a shirt she liked was worth much more than the hundred bucks it took to buy it. I knew we could not spend money indiscriminately, but I was not going to make copper wire stretching a penny either. This philosophy seemed to work well enough to get us nice clothes, new furniture, my shiny convertible, and still leave enough for a down payment on our first house. All in all, we had a lot to be thankful for.

INVITED IN

To be sure, Angela and I were living the world's version of the good life. We had drinks at happy hour, sometimes too many. We stayed out too late, slept in too late, and in general, we did whatever we felt like doing. We did not try to rationalize it or make excuses. We did not pretend to be something on Sunday that was different than the rest of the week. We would try to make it to church most Sundays, but we certainly were not regimented about it. One of the reasons is because Angela and I were coming at this faith thing from two completely different backgrounds. She was raised as a Catholic, and I was raised as a...well...nothing. Since she still wanted to practice her Catholicism, I agreed to go to mass with her. Based on my preference, we also found a Baptist church similar to the one I had been attending with Mom.

I cannot say that either one of us was totally comfortable with the worship style of the other's church. Yet long ago, she and I decided to mutually respect our differing traditions and preferences. In one of our many long talks while still in college, we committed to following our hearts and not choosing one denomination over another just because. Although we knew that that was what most "Christian" couples chose to do, we also knew that it was not right for us. People asked us what we would do if and when we had kids. Our response was simple. We would teach them to love Jesus and let them choose how they wanted to worship. I know this sounded naive to most everyone in our lives, but it was our choice and we put it into practice from the start.

The unfortunate thing about it was we did not really feel like we had a church home. We did not feel like we belonged. In our search for an answer, we went to the pastor of the Baptist church we had been attending. We discussed our situation and asked his advice. He proceeded to explain exactly how he felt about the Catholic faith, that I was the spiritual leader of the family and that I needed to make a decision. With Angela in tears as we left the meeting, I was torn by what to do. Some of the things the pastor said did make sense, but they also kind of ticked me off. I could not see the choice as having to be one or the other. I had no desire to become a Catholic, yet I was not going to force Angela to worship a different way. I finally did make a decision. That was to stick with what we had already agreed. It was not going to be one or the other in our house. We were going to follow the Lord and follow our hearts.

We attended that church a few more times, but we did not join. We even pulled double duty several weekends by going to mass on Saturday evening and services on Sunday. We had plenty of church going on in our lives, yet, more importantly we had God in our lives. I was happy to say that for us His involvement did not end at the church door, no matter which type of door it happened to be. Angela and I took up reading Scripture together and began doing a couple's devotional. I cannot way we did it daily, but it was meaningful when we did do it. The lessons helped us talk more deeply about our levels of faith, where we struggled and how we saw things. Even though we did not always seem to be in the same place on things, we always respected each other's opinion and looked for common ground. The best common ground was the knowledge that God had truly brought us together for a reason. We knew that we were immensely blessed and we thanked Him repeatedly. We also began to realize that going to Him was more important than just going to church.

A TRIAL

Although our social lives and our faith walks may not have looked congruent, we were at least smart enough to know that we could not rely on the good times when times were not so good. Not long after we moved into our first house, Angela started having pains in her side. From what she could tell, it had to do with her mommy parts. The pain grew worse as the weeks went by, so Angela finally decided to go to the doctor. At this point I was concerned, primarily because she had problems in college and the doctors back then thought it might be cervical cancer. It turned out to be nothing, but having the "C" word and the love of my life in the same thought shook me to the core at that time. Of course, that thought was not any more pleasant now either. After several tests and what seemed like years of waiting, we found out it was not cancer, but something completely different. Angela had a miscarriage.

The news knocked us pretty much sideways. It was the last thing we were expecting. We certainly were not expecting to be expecting. What I mean is, while we were not doing anything to keep from getting pregnant, we were not exactly planning it. In the backwash of the news, a slew of emotions swept in that we did not anticipate. There was a child, a baby we would never get to meet. And this baby was going to be ours. How could we mourn for someone we never knew? In addition to this question, I did not know what to do for Angela. She found out she was going to be a mom and then found out she was not all from one set of tests. She took the news well, but I still felt helpless. I felt even more helpless when Angela's deeper concerns surfaced. She shared with me that she was not sure she would ever be able to have kids. I do not think there was any medical reason for her doubt, but she had a strong sense it might be true. I offered in jest that we now knew we could do the first part, but she did not see the humor in it. She went on to explain that her heart for social work and adoption may have meant that we would need to adopt our own children instead of having them biologically. After two years of marriage without something happening, I had a hard time disagreeing.

Yet again, I had very little to offer my bride. I did not want to say "Don't be silly" or "Just get over it." I could tell she had serious concerns. I tried to be there for her and tried not to overreact. We prayed a little and that seemed to help, but what helped the most was a deeper sense that things were going to be all right. We both felt a peace about the situation. We knew we did not have to do anything right away. We felt no leading to look into artificial methods or start looking for a child to adopt. I had the strong indication on my spirit that like everything else, if we could stay relaxed and not try to take control, things would come to us.

In the short term, things at least got back to normal. We continued working and enjoying the good life. Angela left her job and got another working for a Catholic social services agency. She felt at home with the organization and she quickly made a lot of friends. I got a promotion at work and was now making more money than ever. Things were really looking good on the job front, and we had established some great roots in Cincinnati. But as one might expect, our back to normal life did not stay that way for long. Soon after we got settled in our new positions, I broke the news to Angela that Cincinnati would not be our town any longer.

When I Grow Up

Along with my promotion came the opportunity to relocate. I say opportunity with tongue in cheek because neither one of us was excited about moving. Angela was even less enthusiastic when she heard where we were going—Detroit. We had nothing specific against the city, but at the time, it was not at the top of our list. We knew nothing about Detroit other than what most people knew: sports teams, automakers and crime. We knew nobody up there. My only connections were through work and that was the reason I was being asked to transfer. My new boss was a regional vice-president, based out of the motor city. So, like it or not, when he said it would be great to have me there, it was an offer I could not refuse.

I discussed it with Angela and she agreed that it would be an awesome opportunity to advance my career. I was grateful for her support, but I had to laugh when I heard the word career. I never thought of what I was doing as a career. Sure, I had enjoyed some great early success. I had garnered a substantial income. I had even received promotions and accolades. Yet, thinking of this job as a career seemed odd. In reality I pretty much walked into what I was doing. Once I finished graduate school, I started the customary interview process. But in my usual quality vs. quantity, or anything vs. quantity approach, I only interviewed with three companies. Of the three sales positions being offered, I picked the one that paid the most. Such was the beginning of this illustrious career.

I did not have a dream to go into sales or a passion to work in the technology industry, but here I was following that sales job to my third city in five years. When my friends and co-workers congratulated me, all I could give was a half-hearted thank you. I would chuckle and say: "Yeah, the promotion is great, but I still don't know what I want to be when I grow up." The more I looked to the past the funnier my situation became. Being a sales rep was a far cry from the life of a record producer, and being a record producer was now a far cry from what I wanted to be.

The truth was I had realized more about what I did not want to be by this time in my life than what I did want to be. I could not see being in sales or management for forty years and then retiring. I could not see myself doing anything for that long, and at the age of twenty-seven, I certainly was not thinking about retirement. Part of this was because I had only been working a few years. However, there was also something else. It was something I could not fully describe or understand. I had this feeling, like a dull sense that so many other things were happening out there. Where was out there? I had no clue. What I did know was that this feeling had traveled around with me for as long as I could remember. I also knew that my successful career in sales was not satisfying that feeling.

The move to Detroit did not do much for my satisfaction either. It did turn out to be a great opportunity from a job perspective, but pretty much everything else was a loss. We settled for a house that was a lot smaller and a lot more expensive. We said goodbye to a lot of great friends and Angela left a job she really loved. I very much appreciated the sacrifices Angela made, and I knew she was truly proud of and excited for me. Yet this was also very difficult for her. She found another job, but it was not the same. She tried her best to get used to her surroundings and make new friends. We even visited several churches in an effort to establish some faith roots. Unfortunately, none of this was quick to bear any fruit.

RESIDUE

In some ways not knowing what I wanted to be when I grew up was beneficial. It certainly gave me a youthful approach to life. I often felt like a big kid at heart. I tried to not take myself too seriously, and I tried to roll with the trials of life. I was excited to try new things, and I was not afraid of looking silly or making mistakes. This childlike exuberance helped me on the job, and was probably a big reason for my advancement. It also made me popular with co-workers and with subordinates. I could be everyone's buddy but also rally the troops to get the job done when needed. I could make people laugh and help them relax. Whether we were out having a good time or striving to close a big deal, I wanted things to be loose and positive.

That is how I was most of the time, but in many other ways, my carefree approach had negative effects. This "Don't sweat it" attitude allowed me to be brash, condescending, opinionated, and sarcastic—basically, a jerk. Since I did not take much seriously, I expected everyone else to do the same. When I did take something seriously, I had no problem expressing my anger. If I offended someone, I assumed he would get over it. If he did not, it was his issue. I prided myself on being the guy who would say what everyone else was thinking. And if it would bring a laugh, then it was definitely coming out of my mouth. It was very easy for people to know what was on my mind because I told them. If their point of view differed, I did not really care about that either. This approach garnered me some great nicknames through the years like "The shock man" and "Little dude with an attitude." For the most part these were terms of endearment, but they were also flimsy explanations for my abrasive behavior. In several respects, I had not changed much from that smart aleck kid in high school who refused to care.

It was as though the old habits from my youth were intertwined with my youthful outlook. Although I had grown up in some areas, and I now had a lot in life to care about, I still felt the pull to be emotionally disconnected. If I was having fun, even at someone else's expense, it did not matter as long as others were laughing with me. If I was bowling over someone to make my point, it was okay because I was probably right anyway. I felt perfectly justified most of the time, even when I knew I hurt someone's feelings. After all, people teased me. I did not care when guys would crack jokes at my expense. Actually, I took it as an invitation to return the favor. My problem was that I saw everyone as fair game, even if they did not want to play the game. I was not intentionally trying to be hurtful or manipulate anyone's feelings for my own gain, I simply did not hold their feelings or my feelings in very high regard. I liked it when they shared their thoughts, but I also expected them to have thick skin when I cracked jokes. It still seemed like a good balance to me, and it seemed like a great way to stay happy. The only problem was that I did not have it all figured out myself. I had to admit this because I knew I was not always happy.

CHINK IN THE ARMOR

A few days before my birthday I walked to the mailbox, grabbed the mail and walked back. As I sifted though the bills and credit card ads, I noticed an envelope from my dad. Knowing that it was probably a birthday card, I tossed the bills aside and opened it first. I read the short verse and smiled with thankfulness. Then I read through the note Dad had written on the blank flap. It was very heartfelt and at the end he closed with the simple words "I'm very proud of you. I love you, Pop." At that moment a flood of emotions swept over my heart. Before I could react, my eyes filled with tears and I began crying softly. I had no idea what was happening. It was not as if I had never heard my father say those things. Why was I reacting this way to a simple birthday card? As I searched for a reason and tried to sort out my feelings, I realized that there were too many to grasp. Pain, sadness, and frustration mixed with pride, validation and gratitude into a dizzying array of impulses I tried to suppress. It was too much to take. I swiped the keys off the table and drove to a nearby park. I sat on the bench and lit a cigar in an attempt to relax and clear my head. *What was that all about?* I wondered. With each puff I strained to look deeper into my heart for an answer. Though I was not comfortable doing a heart search, I figured I might as well since it had obviously been ripped open. Unfortunately, no great clarity came. I knew it had to do with events from the past, but I could not tell what I was supposed to do with it now. Besides, my relationship with Angela had helped me so much I assumed everything from back then was resolved. Having no answer by the time my cigar was done, I drove back home and called Dad. I thanked him for the card and awkwardly tried to explain to him what had happened. He did not seem to get it, so I just let it go. I chalked it up as a one time thing and figured it would not happen again. I was wrong.

It is a good thing I could let my guard down with Angela, because the next time it happened I was with her. And again, it was on my birthday. It may have actually been a few days after, but nonetheless we realized that my mom had not sent a card or even called on the phone. Now to me, this should have been no big deal because I really did not care about my birthday. I never had. But for some reason, as Angela and I were talking, I burst into sobs again and collapsed into her arms. I cried harder than I had in years, and I was disgusted with myself. I am sure she had no clue what was going on because I certainly did not. There was no reason to react this way about such a trivial matter. Yet we both knew enough to see that I still had things from my past to confront. Her experience as a counselor led her to suggest that I talk to Mom about it. I agreed, but as it was with Dad, I did not know what to say. In both cases, my emotional reaction was not connected to anything I could articulate. Yet I did know that immense pain and sadness were present, and I really did not want to deal with those feelings. It was this type of confusion around my feelings that I tried to avoid. I did talk to Mom and she apologized, but that was as far as it went. This time when I recovered, I was much less sure that it would not happen again. Apparently, the past was still present no matter how bright my future. And though going with the flow had brought me much happiness, I started to realize that it might also bring struggles.

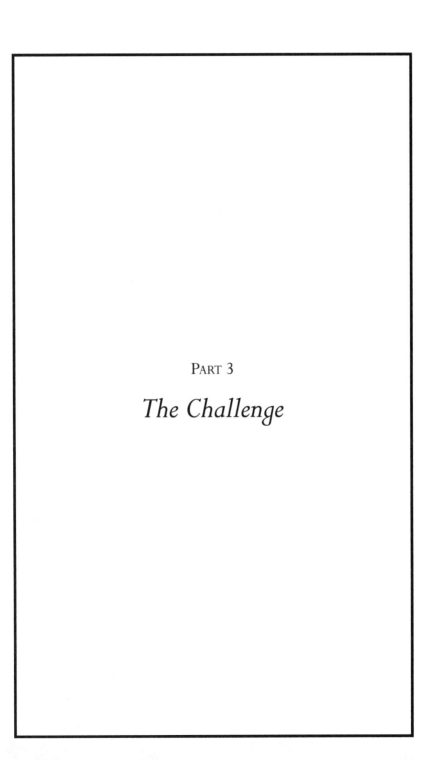

PART 3

The Challenge

Chapter Nine

A Serving Heart

"I thank Christ Jesus our Lord, who has given me strength, that he considered me faithful, appointing me to his service."

1 TIMOTHY 1:12

FATHERHOOD

Our first winter in Detroit was brutal. The smaller, more expensive house we bought had a steep driveway, which made it impossible for our pretty little convertible sports car to make it into the garage. Many nights I drove home from the office, cursing this town, and fearing for my life as I slipped and slid down the icy, snow-packed streets. It was not like Cincinnati. When it snowed in Detroit, it snowed a lot. And the worst thing was that it stayed. It seldom got warm enough to melt, so new snow kept pilling on top. I yearned for the days when I could pull out my flimsy plastic shovel once or twice a year and dust off the drive. Now I was moving what seemed like a metric ton of the heavy powder daily. My work buddies, who all had ridiculously large snow blowers, laughed when I defiantly said I would not get one. But I did consider getting one of those equally ridiculous four-wheel drive SUVs that everyone in Michigan seemed to be driving. It did not matter that neither my wife nor I would be able to see over the steering wheel. The one thing I did know was that the convertible sports car's days were numbered.

Granted, this is hardly a tale of serious woe, but by the time the snow did finally begin to melt in April, Angela and I were ready for a bright spot in our frostbitten lives. What we got was a notice that our lives would never be the same. After three and a half years of patiently waiting, we found out that Angela was pregnant. At first we did not know how to react. We were nervous, excited, scared and almost in disbelief. Understandably, Angela was a little concerned due to our previous troubles. I felt concerned as well, but I was more dumbfounded by the thought of becoming a father. Everything happened so quickly in Cincinnati, I did not have time to give fatherhood much consideration. As a matter of fact, I had never given fatherhood much consideration. Guys do not typically spend their days dreaming about when and if they will have kids, and if so, how many. On the contrary, my high school friends and I used to joke that we probably would not live long enough to procreate the species.

As the news settled in and the doctor confirmed everything was fine, the thought became a reality. I was going to be a dad. Like so many other times in recent years, I was brought face to face with the understanding of how far I had come. I struggled to grasp how the brash adolescent, resigned to living alone, now had a beautiful wife, an amazing marriage, and the beginnings of a wonderful family. It seemed incongruent. It looked to me as though I had led two separate lives. One ended and a new one began without as much as a memo notifying me of the transition. In all honesty, I could not point to any one thing that had allowed for such a drastic change. But I knew the change was not all my doing.

The Band

With plenty to think about and be thankful for, I embraced the notion of being a father. Yet, I also knew I had plenty of time for the notion to become a reality. Angela was not due until December, and it was only August. As the initial excitement faded into the general anticipation of getting to the end, we migrated back to our original routines: working, playing, and half-heartedly searching for a church we liked. We attended mass at a nearby Catholic church, and poked around at a few others, but we felt about as connected to a church community as we did to the Detroit suburbs. We knew finding a church was important, yet it was not a priority at this point in our lives. Then one day, out of the blue, I got a phone call. A guy I worked with named Phil wanted to know if I would be interested in playing the drums in a band his church was starting. It seemed like a pretty specific request, especially since I did not know Phil all that well. Yet we had talked enough for him to vaguely remember that I used to play the drums. The truth is I had not picked up a pair of sticks in nearly ten years, but I guess I still qualified in his book. He said they were going to be doing a contemporary service and were forming a band to lead praise and worship in a Christian rock format. Well, I was a Christian, and I liked to rock, so I said OK.

I hung up the phone laughing to myself. *I just agreed to do what?* I thought. I told my wife and she thought it sounded cool. To me it sounded comical. I had never brought my faith together with my musical abilities, other than to sing hymns during a service. My only experience worshipping with a praise band was at a very polished mega-church I visited with other friends from work. It was one of those places that look more like a movie theater wedged in a college campus than a church. The service was great, but it was not a fit for our worship styles at the time. With that in mind, I carried a high degree of uncertainty into the first rehearsal. I went to the church wondering if I even remembered how to play but comfortable in the fact that I harbored no expectations.

I arrived at the church to find the makings of a classic jam session. That is when a group of musicians get together in an impromptu gathering and start playing whatever they know. I quickly realized we were on to something special that first night. We had musicians of varying ability. And yet, when we started to play, things clicked. I also realized that I had not forgotten as much as I thought. I actually jumped right back into playing as if I had never stopped. I thoroughly enjoyed myself. It was more fun than I could remember having in church. It was also a great rehearsal in and of itself. But there was something more. We had a flow and a connection that seemed larger than the songs we played. This connection and my enjoyment were strong enough to bring me back. I agreed to keep rehearsing with them and, if nothing else, my curiosity was peaked. I definitely wanted to see where this was going.

A CHURCH, A HOME

Yes, this church was putting a band together, but it definitely was not going to be part of a modern, mega-church experience; quite the opposite was true. This band would be pumping out Christian praise and worship tunes in a church that was more that 150 years old! Complete with the official historical marker, and 1800s architecture, this little church on a hill looked more like a museum piece than a place that housed rock 'n' roll gospel. When I saw it for the first time I thought I had gone back in time. I half expected to see the Ingles family worshipping inside, dressed in their finest Sunday-go-to-meeting clothes. And the fact that it was a Methodist church made it even stranger for me. I could not remember ever setting foot in a Methodist church before that day. I did not even know what a Methodist was. But I figured they still worshipped Jesus, so Angela and I started attending.

From day one we both felt loved and accepted. The people in the congregation displayed warmth that made us feel instantly comfortable, despite the fact that neither of us understood the Methodist traditions. We attended the existing service a few times and switched when the contemporary ministry launched. Then, of course, I was not merely attending, I was participating. Admittedly, I felt a little apprehensive. Though I was by no means a pillar of faith, I wanted to be sure we were sending the right message. I did not mind mixing rock music and faith in my life, but my loose Baptist ties made me well aware of the dangers associated with having "secular" elements in the worship setting. I ultimately trusted God to bring me back if I got off in the weeds, and I asked for his guidance as I moved forward.

This was truly a big step for me. I had all the usual performance anxiety, but in a larger sense, this marked the first time I would participate in worship instead of holding down a pew. After the first few Sundays, the nerves subsided and I began to feel the energy and inspiration of the music and of the service itself. Something in me came alive. Suddenly going to church developed a whole new meaning for me. A depth and purpose grabbed a hold of my heart and mind. I now had a reason to go that was much more important than just knowing I should. A team was counting on me to contribute, and we were all contributing to a worthy cause.

I bought into the vision of the ministry which aspired to share God's love and develop fully devoted followers of Jesus. I got involved with all the creative aspects of planning the services. It seemed so simple yet so revolutionary. Though many other churches were doing the same thing, it felt like we were breaking new ground. In that very traditional congregation, we were absolutely blazing a new trail. As one might expect, several people got a little singed by the trail blazing, but we expected everyone to catch on fire. My spirit had certainly been ignited. For the first time, I started to see how my talents could be used for a higher purpose. I became excited to do something I enjoyed, knowing that it might make a difference in someone's life.

LIFE'S OVER

That winter someone made a difference in our lives. The day after Christmas was Sunday. Everything was fairly normal as I got up to get ready for church. The only thing out of the ordinary was that Angela had already been up for some time. She walked around the house breathing strangely and grimacing in pain. She obviously did not feel well. In any other case, I would say the she must have taken in some bad Christmas turkey, but the fact that she was nine months pregnant and due any day meant that something else was up. It was time. I called the guys in the band to let them know I would not be able to make the service, and we headed out for the hospital.

On the long drive across town, I noticed time starting to slow down. Everything in the world seemed to fade until Angela and I were the only two people on the planet. My senses were extremely heightened and my focus was totally on her. I was not anxious or panicked in any way. In fact, an overwhelming sense of peace and calm swept through me so completely that my body was warmed from head to toe. Angela was, of course, focused on other things, but she did not seem to be any more agitated than I was. We quietly drove through the icy rain to the hospital. I checked her in and went back out to the car for the bags. I could not get over how protected I felt. I knew beyond the shadow of a doubt that everything was going to be perfect. I had never felt more right or alive. Assurance draped over my spirit like a thick blanket.

The delivery did go perfectly. From my perspective, it was quick and easy. Granted, Angela did all the heavy lifting, but she came through it with beauty and elegance. At around one o'clock I looked into my daughter's eyes for the first time. "Hello, Gianna." I whispered. As every dad knows, that moment changes a man. She immediately found her way to a new place in my heart. I remember getting lost in her gaze thinking, *Life as I know it is over.* The thought was not a lament or one of regret. It was more an acceptance of tremendous blessing and responsibility. I knew I would never be the same again, and I welcomed the change with open arms.

A few hours after our daughter was born, I wandered by the entrance to the chapel at the hospital. Before I knew what I was doing, I walked in, sat in the front row and looked up at the cross. Immense gratitude welled up in my heart as quickly as the tears in my eyes. The urge to thank God grew so strongly, it was all I could do. That same sense of peace and calm I felt in the car grew even more intense. I thanked God repeatedly and asked Him to bless Gianna. Tears streamed down my cheeks as I prayed for her protection and prayed for her to know Jesus deeply and personally. I asked God to help me be the father she needed me to be. It was the most honest, sincere prayer I had ever offered. I had never felt the touch of God more deeply than at that moment.

In the way that finding my wife allowed me to love as I never had before, becoming a father expanded my capacity all the more. God broke in to provide another powerful, albeit unexpected and un-requested miracle. I had to acknowledge that those miracles were piling up in my life like the treasures of a rich man. That day I felt like the richest man in the world.

UNBALANCED

When we brought our daughter home from the hospital, it still felt like we were the only ones in the world. Except now it was the three of us instead of the two of us. We were excited to start our family, yet like most new parents, we had no clue what to do. And after our parents left, we had to figure out how to care for this beautiful little creature. One of the first things we had to work through was how to get her to sleep. Angela and I knew we were in trouble when our daughter came into the world with her eyes wide open. She did not want to sleep then, and she did not want to sleep now. Many nights we took turns doing laps in the hallway wearing ourselves out and thoroughly entertaining our daughter. I did not miss the sleep that much because I had never slept all that soundly. Angela, on the other hand, could sleep. If sleep were a sport, she would be a world champion. When we first got married, she could sleep in past noon with no problem. Gone were those days.

Motherhood was a rude awakening for my wife—literally. Everything else about being a mom she loved, but the sleep deprivation was really hard on her. This fact coupled with the typical post-partum, emotional roller coaster made for some interesting discussions in our early days of parenthood. Furthermore, we began to discover that our difficulties were not solely based on the physiological. Angela and I had ideological differences on how to parent as well. I found myself in the "let them cry it out" camp, and she was more in the "swoop in and grab them every time" group. We both tried to respect each other's opinions, as always, but now we had a child to raise. The choices we made as parents had life shaping implications. Knowing this made it tough for us to remain relaxed and objective when it came to our daughter. For the first time in our lives together, there was an important issue where we did not see eye to eye.

This created some stressful moments and some arguments. Angela and I were both passionate people, so spirited disagreements were a part of our marriage. Yet we had always tried to resolve them in a healthy manner, and we knew it was critical to do that now more than ever. We prayed for God's strength and guidance and relied on our mutual love and respect to carry us through. Even though I did not always display the utmost love and respect, I knew I could not impose my will without creating resentment. I tried to honor Angela's role as the primary caregiver and I knew that she was stubborn enough to do things her way when I was not around anyhow.

My not being around was another big issue in those days. I worked a full eight to ten hours per day and was starting to spend a lot of time at the church. Since I had become heavily involved in the ministry, I was at the church sometimes two, three or four nights a week. I would have been gone every night if need be. I cannot say I was addicted to serving, but I was definitely committed. Since this was all new to me, I did not know any other way to be. I had never heard of the concept of getting burned out on ministry service. I figured if it was a noble cause, everyone would be on board. I realized quickly that was not always the case. The resentment I tried to keep from our marriage crept in as Angela expressed her concern over my times away. She supported the ministry fully, but she also reminded me that I had a ministry at home to support. I knew she was right. And I knew I now had an added challenge in my life. I had to learn how to balance all of its blessings.

FOR YOU

I guess if a person has a challenge to face, sorting through abundant blessings is a great one to have. I know it sounds crazy, but I truly felt like I had more goodness going on in my life than I could handle. I definitely felt I had more good things than I deserved. It seemed as though I was watching a movie of someone else's life. This screen play told a ridiculously sappy story of an unassuming fellow who haphazardly stumbled into that amazing marriage and beautiful new family along with a fulfilling life of service; all without lifting a finger. In addition, he had great job that allowed him to live comfortably and have nice things. It was all so wonderful. If it really had been a movie, I would have walked out before the end thinking: *What a chick-flick!* But as much as I could not believe a life like this was possible, I had to face the fact that I was living it. And I knew I would not trade it for anything.

During this time, a strange shift took place deep inside me. What was once a random set of events and mishaps I casually referred to as my life began to take on continuity that I could not deny. It was at this point I completely gave up on reflecting how far I had come. There no longer seemed to be a need for it. Not only was the amount of change and resultant blessing far too much to grasp, the culmination of it seemed to bring me purposefully to the present and to the future. The shift came in the way I saw

God working in my life. He was not arbitrarily throwing me blessings to let me know He was a nice guy. Nor was He using these gifts as a way to manipulate me into living a moral life. He was doing all these things with intent. He was doing all these things with meaning and purpose. These gifts and blessings were real, and more importantly, the source of the blessings was becoming real to me. Instead of feeling lucky or having a nebulous sense of appreciation, I knew that I had someone specific to thank. Yes, I had thanked God on numerous occasions before, but now something was different. I started to connect the dots. The randomness of my life and its loosely associated miracles slowly seemed to be taking shape. Things did not feel so random anymore. Things like my salvation, my marriage and my child developed an added significance in light of this newly discovered connectedness. As my clarity increased, I made a rather subconscious decision to take an active role, acknowledging the need to live my life instead of letting life live me. Slowly I became more aware that my life was a gift and I needed to honor that gift by honoring the gift giver.

I am sure these are many of the things I would have experienced at the time of my conversion if I had known what to do or where to go. But now, some twenty years later, I was seeing it all for the first time. I felt trilled to be serving in church. I was excited to be sharing the truth of Jesus Christ with others, and, I was grateful to know that God was at the center of our family. Most of all, I became truly grateful to realize that my Lord had done all these things for me.

Chapter Ten

Man in the Mirror

"As water reflects a face, so a man's heart reflects the man."

PROVERBS 27:19

FAITH ON THE FRINGE

Meanwhile, back at the office, my career stayed in high gear. I continued to have great success and gain great experience. And once I worked my way out of management and back into sales, I started making great money again. Sure, I enjoyed being a manager. When I came out of school, it was actually what I wanted to do. I liked the idea of getting things done by motivating and leading a team, and I was able to do that in part. But all the other corporate stuff like being the middle man, driving initiatives that did not make sense and number crunching, sucked the life right out of an otherwise fulfilling position. I did not even mind the whining and complaining of employees. It broke up the monotony of the day. I used to tell them that my job was to get interrupted. I had an open door policy, and I appreciated the fact that my sales reps could confide in me. What I did not appreciate was that I could make more money on the front line. So when the opportunity presented itself, I made a hasty return to the rank and file.

One thing I wish I would have taken more advantage of in my role as manager/therapist was the opportunity to share my faith. I had never been an in-your-face kind of Christian, and in the work place I was definitely not that way. I openly professed being a Christian to anyone who asked me, but I did not bring it up in casual conversation. Of course, neither did anyone else. I would like to say my lack of boldness was due to intense corporate pressure to be politically correct. Unfortunately, that was not true. In reality, I still liked to have fun, and I still liked playing the game. I knew I would be more relatable if I was the wise-cracking, good time guy. And I have to admit I was good at it. As I said before, I wanted to keep things loose and positive. I could rattle off a classic movie quote or quick one-liner at the perfect time, or at the worst time, which made it even funnier. I could take everyone out for beers and help them blow off steam. I would do whatever was necessary to make people happy and hit the sales goals. As far as I was concerned, work was work and everything else had its place.

I did not feel the need to justify it, but if I did, I could say that I was the sole bread winner in the family. Angela and I had agreed that she would stay home and raise the children. And now that we had a child, she was doing just that. We felt the pinch a little without having her income around for discretionary cash, so I picked up the slack by selling hard and chasing the big deals. I brought in enough for us to live well and have a great time. We tried to live sensibly as well. We paid off a lot of debt. We tried to buy an older used car with cash, but it proved to be unreliable, so I went back to buying new. We also dumped thousands into the stock market like everyone else. Of course, when the market crashed, we lost thousands like everyone else.

The point is that reality continued to happen. Though I experienced all this love and growth in my spiritual and family life, I still had bills to pay and mouths to feed. This drove me to continue keeping my private life separate from my work life. Keeping my faith on the back burner at work had never been a problem before. Most of the time, I did not even know I was doing it. I harbored no need for secrecy and I felt no fear that I would somehow be exposed. It is simply what I felt I needed to do.

Fractured Man

The problem with doing what I felt I needed to do was that I did not find a lot of joy in doing it. One big reason for this was that I did not much care for who I was at work. I had to admit that how I acted on the job did not match up with how I acted the rest of the time. Needing to play the corporate game to bring home the bacon was one thing. Doing the things I was still doing was quite another.

For instance, nobody in my company told me I had to swear like a drunken sailor to keep my job. Yet expletives peppered my speech as if I got paid by the cuss word. I acquired this bad habit from the streets, and from my dad, as a kid. Now it so ingrained itself in my speech patterns, half the time I did not even know I was swearing. And I certainly was not the only person doing it. It ruled as the accepted vernacular around the water cooler, and the boardroom, and the parking lot, and the cubicle. Everyone joined in; but I was particularly fond of the vulgarities. If I grew angry, or riled up, a string of four letter words and improper anatomy references could likely be heard from across the office.

The interesting thing was that even though my colorful speech seemed virtually automatic, I did not find the urge to let it fly at home or at church. It was not only because I knew I shouldn't, it was because I did not have those words on my heart in those settings. I started to wonder what I sounded like to people at work, and I wondered what friends from church would think if they heard me talk that way. At the time I did not feel guilty or convicted; I was merely perplexed as to why there was such a distinct difference.

With alcohol thrown into the mix, it got even worse. Of course, alcohol got thrown into the mix quite often, and I was OK with that as well. I could take it or leave it, but if booze was around, I would usually take it. I did not drink to excess, however, I sometimes had more than I should have before driving home. I was confronted with this foolishness one night after a particularly hard day of work. The sales team and I had finally finished a big proposal and decided to stop by the local watering hole to unwind. One beer turned into several as we celebrated well past the dinner hour. The team parted ways, and without a passing thought I jumped in the car. To compound the situation, I sped out of the parking lot onto the street. It must have been obvious that something was up to the police officer who immediately pulled me over. As soon as I saw his lights, I realized what I had done and what was going to happen. There was no way I was getting out of this. The officer approached my window and asked where I was going in such a hurry. He then, as expected, asked if I had been drinking. Finding no point in lying, I said yes. The patrolman walked to his car and returned a few minutes later, I assumed, to begin the arrest procedure. What he said next stunned me. He suggested that I pull around the corner to the coffee shop and sit awhile with a cup of strong coffee. Still in shock as I took back my license, I uttered a simple "yes sir" and made a beeline for the tiny café.

I lingered over that cup of awful java for more than an hour marveling both at how fortunate I was and how stupid I had been. I admitted that the choices I was making and the way I was acting were the behaviors of a man I did not want to be anymore. The coffee must have been strong enough to clear my head and bring the incongruence of my life in to sharp focus. I vowed not to drink and drive anymore, and I knew I had to start making better choices if I wanted to live outwardly how I felt on the inside.

DAUGHTERS OF EVE

I'll never forget the day we stumbled into that old garage. My cousins and I were clearly trespassing and we knew if we got caught we would be in big trouble. But the door was wide open, which made it way too inviting for a group of small boys to pass up. We kicked around the beat-up old barn for a bit looking at all the worthless junk and loose car parts. We were just about to leave when we noticed a cabinet by the door. Curiosity gripped us instantly. We opened the doors to see what was inside. What we found was all too haunting and all too compelling. We had discovered stacks of magazines, several stacks of magazines, all of them pornographic. We should have been grossed out or scared. We should have gotten the heck out of there, but we didn't. Still in the grip of curiosity, we began thumbing through book after book of some of the most deplorable pictures ever taken. We saw all sorts of people doing things with other people that should never be attempted much less photographed. We laughed at most of it and stared with wonder at the rest. We had no clue what the bulk of it meant, but it left an indelible mark on my mind. I was eight.

By some miracle, I did not become addicted to that stuff, but I was certainly desensitized to it. Over the years, I had several chances to allow material like that into my brain. I usually welcomed it as an odd sort of novelty. With that influence and the sheer fact of growing up in our modern culture, it is no wonder that I struggled to see women in a pure context. I had gotten in a very bad habit of looking at ladies' physical attributes and allowing my thoughts to drift to naturally impure conclusions. Throughout my career, it had been all too easy to entertain customers at gentlemen's clubs where the physical attributes are blatantly obvious.

But now, with all of the changes taking place in my heart, I had to honestly ask myself why I did these things and why I had these thoughts. Though I would never think of cheating on my wife, I now had the words of Jesus clanging around in my mind. If I was committing adultery in my heart, how was that any different? Was that really how I wanted to be?

The duality of my life hit home while at a church leadership retreat. We were engaged in a topic on godly love, when the pastor broke out to talk about the pitfalls of sexual attraction. He discussed how as men we should strive to see all women other than our wives as we see our mothers or our sisters. I was instantly convicted. I knew that was not how I was viewing women in my daily interactions. I had an ingrained, almost knee-jerk reaction to "check them out." While I understood that it would be extremely difficult to stop the initial reaction, I agreed to allow God to deal with the result. I admitted that I needed to give my thoughts over to Him and I needed to trust Him to keep the temptation from settling on my heart. The pastor finished by imploring us to remember that every woman is Gods' child, a daughter of Eve. I kept that image with me as a way to combat the thousands of other images that had attached themselves to my heart over the years.

DONE

Despite all of the friction between my internal self and my outward behaviors, my career was going like gangbusters. In 2002, I finished the year as the number one sales person in the region and made more money that year than I ever had. I won top honors in our annual sales contest. The prize was an all expenses paid trip for me and my wife to an exclusive resort in Southern California. For my marriage, the trip could not have come at a better time. The year prior Angela had given birth to our second child, Isaac, and without missing a beat, we found out we were going to have another in the fall of this year. While we were thrilled to have a son, and we felt blessed that God was growing our family so quickly, it was a lot for Angela to handle. She needed a break.

The trip proved to be a truly great vacation. The weather was great. The resort was beautiful and the time alone was priceless. Plus, we received a ton of awesome gifts throughout the week. All this happened while I was being honored at banquets and award shows alongside my top performing counterparts. It was really an awesome week. And during this awesome week, guess what I realized? I did not want to do this anymore. I was done. Regardless of the wonderful accolades and freebies, I did not feel happy. I think right when I stood on stage being recognized by hundreds of my colleagues was when I decided to quit. Quit to do what? I did not know, but I knew I could not see this being the rest of my life. I had to admit I had not been happy at my job for a long time. I looked at guys who had been doing the same job for decades longer than I had and they did not seem to be happy either. I knew there was no career advancement. I told my boss that they could not pay me enough to take his job. He should have come to work every day wearing a trash bag and a catcher's mitt.

All kidding aside, I felt like I could not make a difference. I had taken a sales job as the path of least resistance, and now I had no idea where that path was going. I grew restless and frustrated. I would say to Angela that I liked being able to come home and cut the grass because at least then I felt like something was getting done. She knew I was not happy as well. She would ask me constantly what was wrong and what was on my mind. Most of the time, while at home, my mind was a thousand miles away. I had this nagging sense of being totally out of phase. When I was at work, I thought about home. When I was at home, I could not let go of things at work. Angela wanted to help, but she did not know how. I felt bad because I wanted to support her, and I felt like I was not stepping up. My performance began to slide at work. I went from the top that year to barely making my sales goal the next. My attitude had gotten so bad, my boss had to call me on it, and rightfully so. I was treating people horribly and having no regard for their feelings.

In general, I acted like an angry man. Even though on the inside, my heart was as open as it had ever been. I was as tired of myself as I think everyone else was. I wanted to have what I felt internally and what I acted like on the surface be the same.

FATHER AND SON

One area of my life where I had begun to live more from my true heart was in my relationship with Dad. For years after he and Mom split up, we had a fairly shallow association. We cared about each other and enjoyed spending time together, but it always seemed like there were a lot of things neither of us could say. This led to us sitting silently most of the time in front of the TV watching sports or adventure movies. It was after one of these stints several years later when something finally happened. I got a call from Dad's wife shortly after we left their house. She asked if I could come back because Dad really needed to talk. I agreed, and when I arrived, I found Dad at the kitchen table crying like I had never seen him cry before. We embraced for a long time. Through his tears he asked for me to forgive him. Through my tears I said, "I do forgive you, Pop."

We sat in the kitchen and talked for a quite a while. The whole time Dad kept repeating that he did not understand how I could forgive him. How could I forgive him for leaving Mom, for breaking up the family, for making bad choices? I tried to assure him, but I sensed him struggling to believe me. The truth was that I really had forgiven him. By God's grace, though I did not seek it, I never harbored deep resentment or anger toward my father. I cared about him too much to shut him out of my life that way. I told him when I asked him to be my best man that he was one of my best friends, and I meant it. I also respected and admired him for the man he was in spite of the choices he had made; and I was grateful for the man he had helped me to become.

From that day forward, our relationship grew deeper and more caring than what I thought a father and son could have. We could still watch sports or movies, or just talk. But, the difference now was that we cherished the time we spent. In all that we did, we were thankful to be together. And when Dad became a grandpa, the celebration was made sweeter because of the genuine pride, joy and love we could express to one another. We found our friendship to be truly remarkable. On several occasions, people said to us they wished they had that kind of relationship with their fathers or sons. We knew that we had something special, and we made a commitment to keep it that way. Dad and I decided that we would take a trip every couple of years, just the two of us. Again, it did not matter where we went or what we did as long as we could have fun hanging out.

At a minimum, we wanted to create memories together. Whether it was hiking in the mountains or the Grand Canyon, or taking a road trip to catch an auto race, the sense of adventure always added to our enjoyment. And the enjoyment added to our thankfulness. Dad and I were both thankful that we took advantage of the opportunity to engage in each other's lives and not stay passive. I was especially thankful to God for helping me realize the special gift I had in a father I dearly loved and who dearly loved me.

STORM CHASING

Storms had always fascinated me. I would sit out on the porch of my grandparent's farm and watch the storms roll in. I loved to watch the clouds darken and shift. I liked hearing the approaching thunder and seeing the wind swinging the trees. When most sane people would seek shelter I would yearn to be out in the elements. There was something raw and real and powerful about a pending storm that would seize my attention. I felt so small yet at the same time connected to something larger. I think I enjoyed the sense of danger, risk and uncertainty that loomed in those black, grumbling masses. Yes, storms were definitely something that could excite me.

That may be why when Angela jokingly suggested I become a weather man, I seriously considered the idea. She was only looking out for my happiness, and we both figured it could not hurt to think about doing something else. I know she did not expect for me take her proposition to heart, but I began to ponder what it would be like to follow a passion like that.

And no, my passion was not to be one of those guys stuck in a studio wearing a bad tie and staring at dots on a screen. I wanted to be one of the crazy people dressed head to toe in rain gear, braving ninety-mile-per-hour winds to bring in live footage of a raging tempest. Or better yet, I wanted to be out in the middle of nowhere in a beat up old truck chasing tornadoes for the sake of life saving science. Sound melodramatic? Maybe it did, but it was a far cry from the shoe box cubicle and sixty-cycle hum of fluorescent lights that I knew. I actually started checking out meteorology schools on line to get an idea of how to break into the business. I quickly ran into some harsh realities. The first was that meteorologists do not make a whole lot of money. The second was that I would probably have to move the family to somewhere like Oklahoma. Nothing against the state, but I had cashed in a lot of chips to move Angela up to Detroit. Now that we had kids and friends nearby, I did not want to propose another move for this harebrained idea. But, the final deal breaker for this dream job came when I could not find a major in tornado chasing.

If a point to all this existed, it would be to say that I was searching. After all, it was great to say that I wanted to move on from my job, but it did make sense to have an idea where I was moving. Granted, the weather man thing may have been far-fetched, but I could see doing something totally different. I did not have to stay in sales, and I certainly did not have to stay in the technology industry. I seriously considered going back to get my doctorate in something like psychology or counseling. Angela and I always had a strong sense that we might end up doing some kind of couples' therapy or relationship coaching. For about a half a second, I thought that maybe I was supposed to go to seminary and get a pastoral degree. But the reality of running church business shook me out of that notion in a hurry.

Despite mulling over all the possibilities, the bottom line was this: finding another job and searching for happiness was not the most important task ahead of me. I had grown too much. There was too much happening in my spirit to be overly concerned with near-term changes and job satisfaction. Something bigger was taking place. I did not have any visibility into it at this point, but I could sense it on my heart and in my soul. It felt like a change in the wind, a change in the wind before a gathering storm.

Chapter Eleven

Big Picture

"See, I am doing a new thing! Now it springs up; do you not perceive it?
I am making a way in the desert and streams in the wasteland."

ISAIAH 43:19

LARGER STORY

I think one reason I liked storms so much was because of the scale. For the same reason, I had a special place in my heart for places like the Grand Canyon and the Rocky Mountains. I enjoyed standing outside in the wide open space, and trying to take in the fullness of what was occurring around me. There was something supernatural and compelling on a level that was hard to articulate. I really wanted to get a sense of the big picture. I had always been a big picture thinker. I had always been a dreamer. In school, I used this quality to fuel my "I don't care" attitude. If I failed a test, I would reason that in a hundred years, it would not really matter. "It is not the end of the world," I was fond of telling myself. But even during those times of obvious over-rationalizing, I had an unshakable feeling that there was a lot more going on than met the eye. If I fantasized about being a rock star or comedian, I believed it could really happen. The fact that I never did anything to achieve those lofty goals and aspirations did not matter. This sixth sense that there was a larger story being told out there stayed with me into adulthood.

When I saw the movie *The Matrix,* this sense came rushing back to me with full force. Most of the movie's wide appeal, apart from the amazing special effects, was the story line that civilization had been enslaved by a complex computer program playing out an artificial life in each of our minds. I am sure most who saw the show could identify with the confused main character as he struggled to grasp the fact that all the mundane aspects of his daily life were simply a ruse to blind him from the truth. I definitely could identify with him. That was exactly how I felt. The film struck a chord with respect to where I was in my faith walk. I had started to realize that reality was rooted in the relationship I had with Jesus Christ. And everything else, especially who I was and how I acted at work, was the wool that had been pulled over my eyes. My focus was changing. The priorities in my life were shuffling.

If *The Matrix* had struck a chord in my life, a book entitled *Wild at Heart* written by John Eldredge played the harmony. The book acknowledges the fact that there is indeed a larger story and that each of us has a place in it. Most importantly, Eldredge affirms that it is God's story, and within this epic tale, we have a battle to fight, a beauty to win and an adventure to live. A clarion call sounded in my spirit as I read these words. The concepts resonated on my heart and through my soul like the strings of a priceless violin. It all made so much sense. *Wild at Heart* helped bring into focus the ways that God had been moving in me these past few years. I remembered how He had shown me the meaning and purpose of the things that were happening in my life. Wrapped in to my roles as breadwinner, father, husband and churchgoer, was an identity I did not yet fully understand. I was a child of God, a warrior for His kingdom, a follower of Christ. These terms which were once vague and distant to me began to take a prominent position. I commenced learning at an accelerated pace. I desired to learn who I was, and I acknowledged a hunger to find out who I could become.

Start Writing

As I sat in my shoe-box cubicle one day listening to the same delightful hum of the overhead lighting, I heard something else that briefly broke through the incessant drone. The sound was that of a soft yet strong voice.

I looked up from my computer to confirm that something had indeed been spoken, but at that moment I realized there was no one around to speak it. I turned around to check the hallway and adjoining room to see if someone had said something in passing. Seeing no one, I turned back to my desk wondering if I had imagined it. While replaying the event in my mind, I realized that what I had heard was not actually an audible voice, but more of an internal one. It came from a place that I could not quite pinpoint, and I knew it was not my usual form of self talk. I reviewed the simple directive in my mind, and I had to admit that I instantly knew the true nature of its source. God had spoken. His calm, confident words to me were "Start writing." In response, I obediently said, "OK," and opened a new document on my computer. I sat staring at the blank page wondering if further instruction would come. None did. In my desire to honor the request, I began jotting down some notes of wisdom I had picked up in recent weeks. Once I had captured everything I could think of, I closed the document and moved on to something else.

I would have been great if I had known to ask God what else He might like to say, or at least ask for some clarity on what He meant by "start writing." Start writing what? Why? How? Any of these questions would have been appropriate; yet I was not at a place in my faith walk where I could have an open dialog with the Creator of the universe. He had never really spoken to me this directly before, and I was not sure what else to do besides what He asked. There had been many times previously where I received a peace on my spirit or a leading during prayer, but never a direct word. It was not something I was seeking and it was not something I had asked to be given.

Maybe I should have been more freaked out or excited, but it seemed so natural I felt no need to overreact. As I said, God was more real to me at this stage of my life than He had ever been. I was beginning to view Him more fully as someone with whom I could have a deep relationship. I still revered Him for His limitless power and might, yet I also had come to truly embrace His son as my personal Lord and Savior. In my evangelical family history, I had heard that term used quite a bit. Now I was living it. Not because I had to, because of a genuine desire to live in Jesus' image. My prayers and requests had become much more direct and fervent. I called on

Him to free me from the obvious character flaws that pervaded my work life. I wanted Him to make me the husband and father that my family needed me to be, and I asked Him to use my gifts and talents however He pleased in service to His church.

For the first time, I was holding Jesus up as the standard by which I wanted to be measured. And as I continued to learn how to fight for His Kingdom and lead by His example, I began to see His blessings and feel His presence more and more each day.

DROPPED IN

Our ministry team attended a church leadership conference in the spring of 2003. It was the second year we had gone, and we loved it. It gave us a chance to bond, fill our spiritual tanks and gather some awesome ministry ideas. One idea that struck us was to have an outdoor, full emersion, adult baptism. We saw the church that hosted the conference perform something similar with hundreds of people getting dunked. It was a very powerful event. Since our church was a traditional, sprinkling only denomination, we thought it would be a good way to change things up. Being in Michigan, we figured it would be good to wait until the middle of summer, and then offer the outdoor service to anyone wanting to partake. The first person to sign up was me.

I had never been baptized. This was not surprising given the way I had come to know the Lord. Yet in recent years, I had grown to understand the importance of baptism as a public profession of faith. Still, I did not feel like it was anything I had to take care of right away. Besides, the few baptisms I had seen were full emersion, so the thought of getting sprinkled did not cut it for me. When we agreed to have the outdoor event, it seemed like the perfect opportunity. So I decided to take the plunge.

The event fell on a perfect day. In typical Michigan summer fashion, it was not very hot and the lake made my teeth chatter just looking at it. The overcast skies did not dampen our spirits, as we could all feel the energy and love in the air. Several people had signed up either to be baptized for the first time or be rededicated to Christ. Many of the guys from my men's group had joined me to celebrate, and a few of them agreed to be go under right along with me. One of the men was my closest brother in the Lord, Phil. His father had passed away only two days prior, but instead of skipping the event to be with his family, he made a point to be here for me and for himself. My family made it a point to be there as well. Mom and Dad both came up, along with Angela's family. With everybody and their relatives together, we had a pretty good crowd. And since it was a Methodist gig, we had plenty of pot-luck dishes to pass.

The ceremony was very heartfelt and warm. Everyone had a look of peace on their faces. When it came time for me to be cleansed, I was ready. I had put it off for so long, and now that it was here, I knew I could not wait any longer. As I slipped under the water and was brought back up, I felt an energy surge through my body. I did not know what to expect, so the surge caught me off guard. All I could do was throw up my arms and yell at the top of my lungs. I truly felt clean. I felt new. I sensed the Lord smiling on me as if to say, "I am proud of you." I could tell He was certain that I did this for Him. And that was exactly why I did it. I wanted everyone to know why I did it.

As I basked in the glow the rest of the day I truly felt blessed. The best way I could say it is to recite a note that Mom wrote in a book she gave me on that day:

> How blessed that you have followed the command of your Lord and Savior in believer's baptism. May you always remember this time of submission, obedience and dedication to your Lord, Jesus Christ, for truly He is worthy.

That absolutely said it all. I wanted to remember all these things and carry them forward into whatever He had in store. For yes, I knew He was truly worthy—worthy to be followed, worthy to be worshipped, worthy to be loved.

WHEELS OFF THE BUS

Serving in church would be great if were not for all the people involved. Throw a bunch of folks together from different backgrounds and different levels of faith, and they can barely get a simple thing like worshipping the Lord done. The problem with being part of a volunteer army was that people could decide not to show up and fight. Even on Sundays when we had a full team and every element was truly God inspired, we could not count on the congregation to show any signs of life. Basically, ministry was hard work. It required effort. It required commitment. And, most importantly, it required faith.

All kidding aside, we actually had some great people with amazing talents showing up week in and week out to glorify the Lord. They did have faith and commitment, but they also had busy lives and families the same as I did. Honestly, we did the best we could with the resources we had, even though most of the time those resources were spread very thinly. Still, God blessed us over the years as we saw lives change and attendance grow. I sensed that we were truly making a difference for the Kingdom. The problem was that as we saw people grow we also saw them go. The ministry was doing well at bringing people in, but they were not staying and getting engaged. Our mission statement was to share God's love and develop fully devoted followers of Jesus Christ. We had to admit that while we were accomplishing the first part of our objective, we fell woefully short on the second. To address this, we started a number of small groups to get people connected and help them advance in their faith. It worked great for a while. My wife and I started a couples group. She also attended a mom's group, and I attended a men's group. It seemed like we were grouping every night of the week. We loved it. The hope and prayer of the leadership team was that we could create an environment similar to what the early Christians experienced in the book of Acts, chapter 2. We gathered together in each other's homes, we shared meals together and we shared our lives. Just when things looked to be rolling, it seemed as though the world crept back in. People got busier and schedules began to conflict. One by one the groups disbanded, and families went back to their normal routines. As the leader of the couples group, I could not help but wonder what I did wrong. I was mad that nobody cared enough to make this a priority in their lives. I felt like I failed.

Not long after this, the ministry took a hit. The director of our seeker service, who was the purveyor of its original vision, began seeing his significant marriage and family issues become public. He left the church discretely, and his direction and leadership went with him. I had little time to feel hurt or betrayed as I reluctantly stepped in to fill the void. I was not called to be the leader of this ministry, but my loyalty and desire to see it continue drove a sense of obligation.

By this time, my taste for serving in the church had soured significantly. I poured my heart out to God, asking what I should do. Should I leave? Should I stay and stick with it? No direct answer came, but I got the indication that the choice was up to me. What He did help me realize was that I could not seek validation from my service or deeds in the church. And I could not allow other people's faith, or lack thereof, to negatively affect my own. By God's grace, He helped me stay focused on the big picture, a picture that thankfully had my relationship with Him at the center.

LEADERSHIP

As if things at church were not in enough upheaval, I had some things to deal with on the job front as well. I was beginning a new year with totally new accounts, a new boss, and a new quota. In essence, I was starting over. That is not a big deal in the world of sales, but since it was happening for the fifth time in five years, I was getting a little tired of the game. So when an acquaintance called me and asked if I wanted to join him for lunch and discuss a business opportunity, I said yes. If it was digging ditches, I would have taken a look. I was looking for something, especially since I still had not found a way to make money chasing tornados.

The opportunity was not digging ditches or chasing tornados, but what I did see was a leadership development training system that made a ton of sense. It was geared around a typical build as you go home based business that I knew nothing about, yet the concepts we discussed had my interest piqued. I was intrigued by the mentorship style of the training system, and I got hooked on the fact that it was founded by Christians. Figuring I had nothing to lose, I joined up and asked to start receiving the leadership materials. As I began working my way through the CDs and books, I got excited by the things I was learning. It had been a long time since I had learned anything of value, and this was all valuable. The material taught tried and true principles of how to succeed in business, along with how to become a leader, how to relate better to others and how to improve your personal finances. In fact, the training system addressed all aspects of life, including faith, family and even fitness. I had never heard teaching that was so comprehensive. It went way beyond undirected motivational babble or rigid business tips and techniques. The lessons contained real-life stories from people who were already successful, stories relating their struggles and pitfalls along the journey. In each case, the mentors explained how the foundations of true servant leadership allowed them to persevere and ultimately achieve their goals and dreams. The trainings also spoke frequently about the need to see a bigger picture and expand our thinking to include more than what we experience in our daily lives. I was way ahead of them.

To a big picture thinker, this was like throwing gas on a fire. My mind was ablaze with all the possibilities and limitless resources these ideas could garner. I could barely contain my excitement. The knowledge that ordinary people had achieved extraordinary results by serving others and leading them to become better rejuvenated my tired heart. It ignited my passion for serving in a way I had never experienced, and it affirmed in me a sense that had been building on my spirit for quite awhile. I was meant for something more.

I did not now if it involved changing careers, starting a business of my own, or going into ministry, but the thought of making a difference on a grand scale haunted me day and night. I felt destined to be doing more than jockeying a desk or a company car. I also knew that if I was to make a change, it would not be in pursuit of my own happiness. In fact, concern for personal happiness had begun to take a definite back seat to other priorities in my life. Not because I was resigned to being unhappy, but because I understood that happiness was a natural result from leading a life of significance. And a life of significance, to me, now sounded like the only life worth living.

WALK OUT

"I have to quit my job." That was all I said as I woke my wife from a dead sleep in the middle of the night. I had not been to sleep. I could not sleep.

I wrestled over the decision for days in my mind. Yet on my heart the decision was made long ago. That night at about 12:30, I had the added finality of hearing, "It is time for you to leave" on my spirit. In response to my statement, Angela said simply "OK" and went back to sleep. It was Tuesday night. On Wednesday morning I resigned.

After ten years, three cities and seven different positions, I called it quits. I was done. I know I said I was done over a year earlier, but now I was really done. I do not know what took me so long to actually make the jump. I suppose that amount of time was needed for the desires of my heart to shift from what I wanted to what God wanted. I am sure I could have quit at any point, but it was nice to have the assurance that the Lord felt I was ready. Apart from the spiritual peace, there was no earthly reason why I was leaving. It certainly was not because I had another job waiting in the wings. To be truthful, I had nothing lined up at all. No leads. No contacts. No list of open positions. On top of that, we had recently been blessed with our second son, Luke. I was walking out with zero understanding of how I would provide or what I would do next.

As news spread around the office, co-workers filed by my desk to confirm the report. Invariably, they asked the same two questions: "Where are you going?" and "What are you going to do?" When I answered "Dunno" to both, they would stare at me incredulously, searching for something to say. In most cases, something like "Good luck" or "I wish you the best" tumbled out for lack of anything better. A few hearty souls told me they admired my guts and courage. They had the look of longing on their faces. It was as if to say they wished they had the same level of gumption. One guy whom I really respected said, "You'll be back." We both laughed as he said it; because we had seen many others leave and return. And while I could not rule out that possibility, I highly doubted it would ever happen. I had grown too much, learned too much, and seen too many new possibilities. Everything this job represented seemed like a compromise to me. Though I was thankful for what it provided me over the years, I wanted to see what lay beyond the comfy cubicle.

It may have been this spirit of adventure that gave my departure a mystical quality. When word got around to the other offices, a buzz started that seemed out of proportion. People could not believe someone was actually breaking free. I felt like a prairie dog leaving the pack to go face down the coyote. I could almost hear everyone barking "You can't go out there!" Depending on who gave his or her opinion, I was brave, foolish or crazy. Many thought I was leaving under protest because our company was requiring the sales people to work union jobs during a labor dispute. I let that rumor float around since it sounded brash and defiant, but that was not why I was leaving. I was leaving out of honor and obedience. Two words that may not have meant a lot to me in the past, yet lately they had become important enough to stake my livelihood and my family's well being on them.

I was honoring God's word and being obedient to His instruction on my spirit. He said go, so I was going. I think it was intentional that I did not know where. I did know, however, that He was going to be there with me. I had come to a point where I wanted my direction to follow His will. There is an old saying that says: "Leap and the net will appear." My foot was now over the edge and the free fall was eminent. Oddly enough, on my last day at work, a huge storm ripped through the area. As usual, I had to watch it come in and, like always, I yearned to be out in it.

Chapter Twelve

A Question

"So I say to you: Ask and it will be given to you; seek and you will find;
knock and the door will be opened to you."

Luke 11:9

Brave New World

I think I looked back, maybe once. But after that, it was full steam ahead. I
rolled into the next phase of my life with a passion and hunger that I had
never experienced. The world blossomed right before my eyes. I felt like I
was seeing everything for the fist time. Colors, once pale, now appeared
deeper and more vibrant. Textures grew richer in detail and intricacy. I had
a heightened sense of awareness. Time seemed to slow down and objects
appeared to move in perfect orchestration with one another. The drone of
a busy street transformed into a symphony of melodic sounds that filled my
ears with inspiring music. I imagined I could reach out and touch anything
around me, even the sky if I wanted. The big picture now looked to be
within my grasp. I was part of it, and it was part of me. I felt completely liberated, set free. A ton of bricks toppled off my shoulders. The stress lifted
from my chest as if a sumo wrestler had been standing on it and decided to
move. I could breathe again, and I breathed deeply. The air smelled sweet,
light and fresh, like a highland meadow after a spring rain. Life-giving energy
filled me up more and more with each passing breath. My pulse quickened.

My mind raced with thoughts of new adventures. A desire burned inside me to make a heroic difference in people's lives. Excited did not begin to describe how I felt, and all this happened on the drive home from the office! It was surprising that, at the outset, I experienced so much excitement without any fear or doubt. After all, I had just walked away from the family's only source of income with no direction on what to do as an alternative. I looked only toward the future, a future no more visible to me than my next step. When uncertainty, anxiety, or even panic would be the typical reaction in this situation, I displayed peace, assurance and enthusiasm. One could even describe me as possessing a confident swagger, which bordered on cockiness. And while a cocky arrogance may have bolstered me in the past, the humbling presence of Someone much more powerful was driving me now. I think that was why I was so excited to begin with. The reason the world looked so new and amazing was because I now more fully saw God in it.

I saw Him in everything. I could sense His masterful work in the beauty of creation. I felt His powerful touch in the warmth of the sun and in the brush of the wind against my face. I gazed upon the depth of His love and the fullness of His image in my children's eyes. Though I had acknowledged God in these things before, there was presently a sameness that surpassed any of my previous experiences. The Father of all this beauty, depth and majesty was also the Father revealing Himself to my spirit, speaking to my soul and giving me guidance day by day. I sensed His desire to show me so much more; even things I could not understand. Yet, along with my nearly unbearable excitement I felt a small tinge of patience. Something on my spirit whispered: "It's OK, there is time." As a calm feeling washed over my soul, a knowing smile crossed my face. I consented on my heart to let God reveal the future according to His timing, and I thanked Him for helping me to realize I did not need to conquer the world that afternoon.

SECURITY BLANKET

During this time, my reliance on God reached a new level. Not only was I seeing Him in everything, I wanted Him to be in everything. I brought every aspect of my life before the Lord. I prayed for Jesus to be the center of my marriage, to protect the kids and to make me a better version of His image. I also asked Him to bless this time and lead me to wherever He wanted me to go. They were honest prayers. I held nothing back. I truly desired to follow the Lord's will in my life. I knew He had given me this time and I treated it like a special gift. I sought to honor Christ by continuing to serve and by being open to His guidance.

I stayed on at the church, did my best to lead our contemporary ministry through lean times and a change in pastors. The Lord blessed us as new volunteers slowly came on board and joined in helping us touch people with His truth and love. Away from church, I developed a love for reading that I never had before. I read everything productive I could get my hands on: Christian books, business books, leadership books. I devoured motivational and history books, along with biographies. I had an insatiable thirst, not only for information, but also for true wisdom. It was just like being back in school, except for the love of reading and thirst for wisdom things I mentioned.

In addition, I was able to serve my family. I helped Angela haul the kids to preschool, got some jobs done around the house, and put in some quality time with everyone. As a bonus, I lost nearly twenty pounds thanks to the lack of stress and to chasing around three kids. For the most part, everything looked perfect, but there was one tiny exception: No money.

Yep, the thing I never really cared much about was something that I could not ignore. I needed to find income from somewhere; and since I was doing the whole live–a–Christlike-life thing, robbing a bank was out of the question. I needed to get another job. I knew I would have to eventually, but I was not all fired up to get one right away. As I said before, I was not even sure if I wanted to stay in sales or stay in the information technology industry. I enjoyed the idea of having my own business, but in spite of all the training, I was not yet making enough money at it. Regardless, I had to do something, and whatever it was, it could not come too soon for Angela.

Since the time I told her I had to quit, she had remained very supportive of my decision. She understood I was unhappy, and she insisted that she wanted me to be happy. She simply wanted me to move on to what would make me happy and pay the bills very quickly. I believed her and I was very thankful for her support. I also could not blame her for growing a little impatient. See, the simple rule is: You cannot mess with mama's security. Although we were doing quite well financially, when the comfort of steady income was disrupted, warning flags went off in Angela's world. I did not see the flags because I knew that something would present itself in time. Though not complacent, I was content to be secure in God's provision. Angela, however, was not going through a lot of the things I was experiencing. She needed something more concrete than the assurance that God would provide eventually. Do not get me wrong, she had a strong faith, but she also believed in faith in action. Angela felt that if I reached out in faith, God would provide a new opportunity. I agreed. I got the resume cleaned up and dug out my contacts. With all my newfound confidence, I was sure that something would turn up quickly.

CARROT

Before I left my job, I told some friends from other companies I was leaving. As is the custom, they said they would keep an ear out for positions that might be posted. Sure enough, not too long after I left, a guy I knew at a large networking products manufacturer called me about a job that was open in Detroit. The job was a good fit for my background, so I sent in my resume. When I got a call for an interview, I noticed a twinge of excitement stir in my gut. This was a great company, one of the world's most admired and respected. To work for them meant having a coveted position and an even more coveted salary. I quickly became enamored with the challenge of making it through their very arduous interview process. I brought the opportunity before the Lord with a very nonchalant attitude. I do not think I was being irreverent; I simply did not want to assume anything or cloud what He might say. I knew enough to understand that the excitement I felt might easily override any guidance God would provide. I also understood that this excitement might be part of His guidance. Without a specific leading either way, I laid the job and the interview at His feet. I prayed that the

Lord's will be done, and I asked Him to help me bring glory to Him, regardless of what happened.

The first interview went very well. I was nervous but confident. As these things go, one can seldom tell what the person is thinking on the other side of the desk, but I felt that I was true to myself and I did the best I could. When they asked me back for a second time, my excitement grew from a twinge to full-fledged butterflies. I started to believe that I might actually work for this company. I also realized I might accomplish what very few others had done—walk in, off the street and get hired. That kind of thing rarely occurred at this place. They usually stole the best talent from other companies, which meant they could be very selective. After the second interview, which also went very well, we began to discuss salary and bonus plans. At this point, the butterflies in my stomach transformed into stars in my eyes. I seldom got worked up over money, but this was good money. The total compensation package eclipsed anything I had ever seen. I stayed calm on the surface and told my friends things like: "Yeah, the money's good. We'll see what happens." On the inside, I brimmed with anticipation like a kid at Christmas. I could hear my inner voice saying "Ooooo, goodie, goodie!"

When I discussed the position with Angela, she obviously shared in my enthusiasm. She was proud of me for doing well, and she nearly danced a jig when I told her the income figure. I had mentioned this company to her many times in my previous job, so she understood that this was a great achievement. Her zeal for the opportunity became so infectious, it caused my eagerness to go over the top. I was proud that she was proud. I reveled at the chance to make amends for the turmoil I caused by quitting in the first place. I wanted this job.

The next two interviews seemed to be almost a formality. And before long, I had an offer letter in my possession, awaiting my signature. At that moment, I again lay everything on the table. Yes, I wanted this job in theory, but did I really want this job? The position would be very demanding, and it would create a very busy lifestyle. In addition, it was in an industry I had given strong consideration to leaving. I tried my best to set aside the prestige and the allure of great money in order to make an objective decision. With no clear answer surfacing, I turned back to the Lord in prayer. I asked Jesus to show me the direction He wanted me to go. Still, no answer came. But what I did receive was a strong sense of peace and grace on my heart and spirit. I took this to mean that the decision was up to me. The freedom to make my own choice was actually a little unsettling. I did not expect the Lord to give me such latitude. Nonetheless, I thanked Him for His graciousness and His blessing. I also committed to honor Him with my decision. I signed the offer letter and started my first new job in ten years. Our family was now back among the financially respectable, and Angela was thankful to have the burden of uncertainty lifted.

BOLD LOVE

I stood in the auditorium, lost in the music as the worship director led the five thousand person congregation in a moment of prayer. The song being sung was something to do with drawing close to the Lord or feeling Him near. It was a song we had sung numerous times in our own service, and I meant it every time. On most occasions, I felt my spirit move as the soulful words echoed through the sanctuary. This time, my spirit moving was not all I experienced. As the music quieted down and the director began his prayer, someone very lovingly came up beside me put his arm around me. My body instantly filled with a deep warming energy. My chest expanded as an involuntary breath drew in to revive me from head to toe. I could feel the tremendous weight of a powerful arm draped over my shoulder, yet at the same time, my feet seemed to lift off the ground as if I was taking flight. The presence of who had joined me was so unmistakable I did not even turn to look in His direction. It would not have mattered. There was no one physically there anyway.

These types of experiences in recent years helped me realize I was definitely in a relationship with someone real. God was revealing Himself to me in various ways through prayer, Scripture and worship. And in every case, things looked to be drawing me back to the simple verse in the Bible that states: "God is love" (1 John 4:16). While I saw this demonstrated in my life numerous times I had not experienced it in personal ways until recently. During my time off, I had been making a commitment to spend more time in prayer and reading the Bible. Some of this came from the necessity of being involved in ministry and leading small groups, but the true nature of my commitment stemmed from my desire to spend time with the Lord. For me, faith had long ago shifted from "have to" to "want to." I was not doing anything in my spiritual life out of obligation. Yes, I was trying to be obedient, but I was also focused on being loving. It just seemed like the right way to be. Since God had been so loving toward me, the least I could do was be that way with Him.

The more I pursued this closeness in relationship the more God changed my perception of Him. Like feeling His presence during the worship service, or sensing His spirit in many other ways, the Lord looked to be blessing my honest commitment by showing me His true nature. Specifically, He showed me that He was not only a God of love; He was a God who loved, who loved me. This came through loud and clear while driving in my car one day. I had turned off the radio and begun to pray as I was trying to do more frequently. I gave thanks for the usual things and prayed for a few people that were on my heart. Then suddenly I felt the urge to ask a question. I do not know what prompted it, but in a plain, childlike tone I asked, "Lord, do you love me?" Almost before I finished the question, I heard a definite response on my spirit: "Yes, I love you deeply, my son." I was instantly overcome. The reply was so strong and true; my heart broke and leapt for joy at the same time. I started crying and had to wipe the tears away quickly to keep my eyes on the road. Without hesitating I responded by saying "I love you too."

In a simple yet profound exchange, God showed me His love for me as an individual. And at the same time, He taught me a valuable lesson: acknowledging love and sharing love are two different things. Of course I knew in my mind that He loved me. As the Sunday school song says, "The Bible tells me so." I also knew that His love was displayed when Jesus died on the cross. Yet when He made the effort to tell me directly, a closeness and connectedness enveloped my heart. I was filled with gratitude at His personal care for me. He knew that I needed to hear it, and I realized that He liked to hear it too. That day I decided to tell God I loved Him every time I talked to Him.

You Matter

The Lord's kind and gentle words in the car that day anchored themselves in my spirit in a way I could not describe. But instead of merely thanking God for what He said and moving on with life, I chose to stay. It may sound confusing, but up until that time, I would go to Christ, thank Him and pray to Him, and then depart. It seemed to be a back-and-forth kind of interaction. After settling into the fullness of His statement, I discovered that going back and forth was not good enough any longer. I desired now more than ever to move closer to Him and explore the depth of this love He had expressed. While I could have so easily said, "Yep, Jesus loves me" and left it there, I am grateful I did not. Christ had obviously honored my commitment to Him by touching me in a powerful and very personal way. I, in turn, tried to honor Him by giving Him a place of primary importance in my heart and my life. Along with bringing everything before Christ, I was now placing nothing ahead of Christ. He was at the core of all my thoughts and daily activities. His life and teachings came alive to me as I poured through the Bible. Simple verses like "Jesus wept" (John 11:35) showed such an unlimited, immeasurable love, I found it hard to comprehend its fullness. What did translate from those pages to my heart was a realization that the love exemplified back then was the very same love I felt today.

The struggle to wrap my mind around this realization consumed my thoughts on a long drive to one of my first sales calls. I took advantage of the miles to bring my struggle before the Lord. The more I prayed, the more one single question sliced through my thoughts with a searing pain. Why? Why did Jesus love me like this? The pain moved from my mind to my heart as I became fully aware of my unworthiness. My chest ached as if it had been caught in a vice. Now the question raged inside me with a deafening tone. I began to weep, and again I fought to keep my eyes on the road as it whirled by at highway speeds. I told Jesus I was so sorry, and I begged Him to forgive me. Still, the question remained. It forced its way to the surface as I cried out, "Lord, why do you love me so much?"

The answer came back low and calm: "Because you matter to me." My pain instantly transformed into disbelief. In shock from His response, I quickly replied: "How can that be? I'm not worthy!" What Christ whispered next shocked me even more. "No, you're not worthy." He said. "You're worth it." By this time, tears had flooded my eyes. I was driving blind, but I did not feel concerned. All I could feel was the tremendous warmth and depth of God's love. It flowed over me in wave after cleansing wave. I felt so humbled by His power yet completely validated by His grace. At that moment I knew Christ had truly done it all for me. He became so real and close to me, I should have switched to the carpool lane.

All remaining pain and disbelief turned to joy as I began laughing through my tears. I managed to keep the car on the road and slowly regain my composure. I took a few deep breaths while still chuckling over what had happened. I was amazed by God's care and concern. My spirit felt heavy yet alive with a new understanding of true love. I was now absolutely convinced that staying with Christ was what I needed to do. And I reasoned that if I stayed with Him long enough, he might not cause me to cry so much, at least not while I was in the car.

Do You Want It?

I made it through the sales appointment without bursting into tears or laughter. And I was fairly certain the customer did not realize he was meeting with a crazy person. Honestly, even if he had picked up on my severe imbalance, I would not have cared. I was no longer concerned about how people saw me. For years I claimed that I did not care how people viewed me or my behavior. But the truth was I could act like I did not care as long I ultimately knew everyone approved. I am not saying I was a people pleaser—far from it. I simply wanted to be admired and respected like anyone would. We had studied this in depth in my church men's group. As we continued to go through the concepts in *Wild at Heart,* I learned that what I was doing before was looking to the people in my life to answer the question of my worth. Yet now that I understood how important I was to God, I did not feel the need to seek acceptance or validation from people around me.

This fueled my desire to seek Christ to an extent which blew away everything I had felt thus far. My hunger for Him advanced into full-fledged starvation. Jesus continued to pervade my thoughts and my feelings. I went to bed thinking about Him and woke up thinking about Him. If someone had called me a Jesus freak, I would have thrown up my hands and added a big "Amen!" But, the funny thing was that nobody did call me that or anything close to it for that matter. Quite candidly, I do not think people could see much of change in me. I was not standing on the street corner with a bull horn or a sandwich board. I did not go to any ballgames with a big "John 3:16" sign, and I most certainly did not slap a bunch of Jesus-y bumper stickers on my car.

I am not making fun of anyone truly called to do these things, but I did not feel compelled at the time to rush out and share my numerous revelations with an unsuspecting world. What I did feel compelled to do was give as much time to the Lord as I possibly could. I got so worked up in my desire to seek Him that I actually committed to spend time alone with Him everyday! This may not seem like much, but for me it was a huge step. Up to this point, I would usually pray to God while doing something else: driving, showering, or sitting with others in services and small groups. Yet, now in addition to all that, I was going to seek Him alone, by myself, with no distractions. At first it was extremely difficult. Even if I was not physically with someone or doing anything, I brought so many distractions with me, I could barely concentrate. Slowly, however, I began to get more comfortable. And sure enough, I heard God break through with a monumental question.

I was alone, sitting in my living room with my Bible open. Though I did not have to worry about wrecking the couch, the Lord was gracious enough to prevent me from another violent emotional reaction. This time His strong, confident voice simply caused me to look up from my reading and focus on His words. Very conversationally God spoke the question to my spirit: "I have more for you, do you want it?" I continued to pause as the words sank deep into my soul. The further the words sank, the more pressure they exerted on my heart. I knew this was no casual question. It was not like my wife asking me if I wanted more ice cream. I did not know exactly what the Lord meant by more, but I clearly understood that my answer was of critical importance. The weight of the question caused me to recoil. I was unsure. Did I want more? If so, what would I have to do to receive it? God's words came so out of the blue, I did not feel ready to respond. The response on my spirit was: "Can I get back to you on that?" Through the silence that lingered, I understood that the ball was squarely in my court.

PART 4

The Leap

Chapter Thirteen

Wasteland

"Then Jesus said to his disciples, 'If anyone would come after me, he must deny himself and take up his cross and follow me.'"

MATTHEW 16:24

BACK IN THE RACE

Ah, corporate life, is there anything so sweet and joyous? Seriously, I was glad to be working again. I enjoyed being back in an office, even though I drove over an hour to get to this one. I appreciated meeting all my new co-workers, and learning how this machine worked from the inside. This company was truly a machine. If one was looking for a fast-paced, high energy career, this was the ideal environment. The place was chock full of top performers. All of them were running hard to make big money and have great success. I had never experienced a work culture where the people so uniformly drove toward excellence. Everyone ran at an incredible pace. Yet even more miraculous than the pace was fact that everyone seemed to be running in the same direction. This created an atmosphere in which expectations were not only met, they were consistently surpassed.

I bought into the idea that the company was truly trying to make the world a better place through technology. Ever since college, a desire to help people communicate better remained on my heart. I justified my decision to sell technology by believing my products and solutions could do that.

For the first time in years, my belief was rekindled, and I once again felt I could make a difference by bringing people face to face; or ear to ear, or at least, mouse click to mouse click. It was great to be part of an organization that shared in this noble endeavor while making huge profits in the process. As the cliché states, I was definitely drinking the corporate Kool-ade.

The only issue with drinking the Kool-ade was that it seemed to be coming out a fire hose. Since running hard was the accepted culture, I hit the ground with my feet moving as fast as they could. I was expected to learn quickly with very little direction or training and begin contributing immediately. I had to ramp up on product knowledge, company policy and go-to-market strategy, all while relaying those things directly to my customers. I did not mind the learn-as-you-go approach, but this was more like flying the plane as you built it. Corporate directives were very clearly communicated, and the requirement was that they be executed immediately. One of my co-workers called it the "ready, shoot, aim" approach. Others reassured me that it would take about six months to get everything figured out. I was beginning to understand what they meant. One of the first things I realized was that whatever anyone did, they did not stop running. In fact, if people had any uncertainty on what to do, they simply ran harder. I knew this would be the case when I signed on, so I gladly joined the herd at breakneck speed. I could not make the big bucks if I was not willing to put in the effort, and the big bucks were part of what led me here. As my pace quickened, I found myself feeling sorry for the poor schleps at other companies. I was excited to be part of the sales elite and feel like my significance was worth the sacrifice.

ROAD WEARY

A big part of the sacrifice was that I did not get to be home that much. I mentioned that the office was an hour away from our house, but in this job, I was not at the office that much either. I covered a sales territory of two states. Many of the locations I needed to visit were too close to fly, so I put in a lot of windshield time, driving to remote cities and small towns. I didn't mind the drive time, other than the fact that it was time away from the family. This may not have been much of a burden in most families, but for us, it was a big adjustment. We had always valued our quality time together, and we came to cherish it all the more during my time off. I went from being at home full time to being at home no time. Many weeks I was gone several days in a row. And even if I was in town, I often had evening commitments that put me home well after the kids had gone to bed. I hated to leave them on Sunday nights or leave in the morning before they woke up. It was tough on me, but I know it was tougher for Angela and the kids. Angela did her best to run the household as a single mom, and the kids were forced to go with the flow.

Unfortunately to our kids, going with the flow often meant going into overflow. Gianna, Isaac and Luke had each inherited the best parts of our strong personalities, so clashes and conflict were a regular occurrence. It was usually nothing more than sibling rivalry or whining and manipulation, but when Angela was left to deal with it all day every day, it began to take its toll. While at home, I noticed that the kids seemed to gang up on her. I know it was not intentional, but kids do tend to be like sharks. If they smell blood in the water, they know it is time for a feeding frenzy. If Mom let one thing slide, they assumed it was open season on getting their way. I picked up on this immediately and began chiming in as the voice of reason, if not the voice of correction. I felt guilty for not being around, so I overcompensated by trying to rescue Angela. This, of course, seldom worked. The kids struggled with the inconsistency and Angela viewed my overreaction as a judgment that she lacked control over them. As a result, we had some interesting family interactions which would hardly be categorized as quality time. I somehow failed to realize that the house did not burn down during the long periods of time I was gone. Angela might not have been holding the line the way I would have, yet she managed to keep the kids happy and safe while I was out conquering the world.

Being on the road a lot did have some upside. I got to spend a great deal of time with the Lord. I could pray for all the people in my life, bring all of my cares and concerns to Him, and even sing worship songs to my heart's content. With no one to talk to besides work people on the phone, I found myself talking to God quite a bit. More importantly, I found myself listening quite a bit. The Lord was not filling my ears with chatter during this time, but I felt Him much more clearly on my spirit. I became very aware of the difference between my inner voice and His instruction. I started to see, hear and feel the numerous ways God communicates with His children. I began taking my Bible with me on every trip. Scripture continued to come alive as I was able to read in the frequent solace of my hotel room. A richness and depth was added to our relationship daily and His blessings became more and more apparent. The only minor glitch was that pesky question He would gently remind of whenever I opened my heart.

Spinning Up

I guess when God asks if someone wants more, He probably expects a response. For several reasons, I still was not ready to give one. At the top of list was the understanding that He was offering a lot more. The initial weight of the question continued to grow, which made me all the more hesitant to say yes. I had no further clarity on what the Lord was offering specifically, and that added to my reluctance. Something very big and unknown had been placed before me.

In addition to the sheer magnitude of the offer, the realization that more did not just mean more riches and abundance also set in. The Lord was not asking to be my personal genie in a bottle, granting all my earthly desires with a wave of His mighty hand. More meant great sacrifice. More meant a need to do things I would rather not do. I am not referring to a command to sell all my possessions or move to Africa. Again, I did not have that insight, but clearly the question came with a significant requirement. Yes, the Lord did have more for me, but He was also asking more of me. This understanding came with no sugar coating and no polish.

I pictured myself standing with my toes hanging over a vast precipice. It would be cute to say I had a devil on one shoulder and an angel on the other disagreeing about what my next move should be, but nothing nearly that black and white transpired. Instead, my mind, heart and spirit seemed to be spinning around the question at ever increasing speed. At any given second, I could simultaneously be thinking, *Oh yeah, I want to go there* and *What are you, nuts?* Mixed in with these thoughts was a truckload of emotions: excitement, fear, joy, worry, elation, panic and doubt. These thoughts and feelings produced a knotted mess of reactions that nearly paralyzed me and stopped my faith walk dead in its tracks.

Right at this point, something astounding occurred to me. I did not have to do anything. I did not have to answer the question or accept the offer. I could stay there with my toes on the edge, admiring the view and contemplating what might be waiting out in the great expanse. I could even turn back; forgetting all that I had seen and experienced. The choice was completely up to me. Though God had been gently reminding me of the question, he was not forcing me to respond. I also understood that even if I said yes, I could change my mind at any time. The requirement that lay on my heart was one I had to willingly receive.

God's abundant grace and freedom through all this was astounding. Not only had He taken the time to offer me more, He was waiting patiently for me to make my own decision. I could hardly believe, yet again, how personally and individually He was demonstrating His love and care. He told me previously that He loved me and that I mattered to Him, now he was proving it. And the fact that Jesus did not have to prove it made it all the more meaningful to me. While I still was not sure that I could take the big step, I knew there was no way I could turn back now.

ENTER THE BOY

It was at this moment in my life that God introduced me to the lost boy. The fullness of this intense vision was too much for me. In a moment of complete spiritual and emotional release, I lay on the floor of my hotel room in a heap, sobbing uncontrollably. I was completely overwhelmed. I felt myself in that boy, and at the same time, I felt the irresistible urge of a father to protect his child. I was frozen with fear and uncertainty. The boy was frozen as well, overcome by the same emotions. Finally, after what seemed like hours, I heard a calm but powerful voice say, "Go get him." With all the strength I could gather, I uttered through the tears, "How, Lord? How do I go get him?" No immediate answer came, but what did come was clarity into a new aspect of my faith life: confrontation. What I had already perceived as a heaviness stemming from God's question had now been confirmed as a specific need to deal with some big stuff.

The confusing thing was that I thought I had already dealt with things from my past. Through earlier teaching and from numerous mentoring sessions with Phil, I had learned enough to allow God access to those areas in my life which needed healing. I dealt with the divorce, forgave my parents and felt a measure of peace that a significant wound on my heart had been healed. But this abandoned boy vision was something totally different. It seemed deeper, more rooted and more complex.

In addition, the way the Lord brought me to it seemed almost stern and matter-of-fact. I felt very vulnerable and even a little bit betrayed. As the vision sank in, I felt as though God had attacked me from a side door. In the months prior to this experience, I had sensed a significant strain on my spirit, but I managed to pull back from it because I did not want to "go there." And now I had been snookered by pressing into the sadness of someone else. The whole encounter was dramatically different from the warm and loving revelations God had shared with me during those same months. The Lord's attitude toward me this morning settled on my spirit as much more of a "tough love" type of exchange.

I have to admit I found myself licking my wounds a bit the rest of the day. I do not mean to say that my feelings were hurt, but I definitely began to form a new perspective of the costs involved with the Lord's offer. I was ready to accept the more obvious costs of following Christ: deny my flesh, flea from sin, be in the world not of the world—all the usual commands. I even accepted the fact that choosing this path meant engaging in direct spiritual warfare. Yet, the conflict and confrontation represented in the vision went beyond resisting Satan and disciplining my spirit against external forces. The longer I thought, the more I understood that my willingness to face the "big stuff" was going to directly affect my ability to rescue this child and my ability to draw closer to Jesus.

As this realization settled on my heart, I felt a steely determination rise up inside me. The image of that little child standing scared and alone, frozen in time, lit a fire in me that I could not contain. Though I had no clear direction on how to bring him back, I vowed to do whatever was necessary to rescue the lost boy.

ALL IN

On the heels of this earnest commitment, my faith in Christ seemed to double overnight. In the days that followed, I struggled to discern why the vision had been shown to me. I continued in my obedience with consistent alone time, prayer, worship and meditation on His Holy Scripture. Still no guidance came, but even that did not trigger the usual frustration or discouragement. I knew I was in unfamiliar territory. The incredible power of what I had seen gave me a glimpse of what may indeed lay ahead. I also realized that God was not trying to trick me when he drew me into the vision. He was pursuing me. In His care and creativity, He was drawing me in and calling me on to all that He had for me. With His masterful hand and His limitless grace, He was also preparing me for a great battle and an unbelievable adventure.

As the fullness of His intent unfolded, it became abundantly clear that my own strength, determination and effort were going to be woefully inadequate if I chose to say yes to the question. I also realized that accepting God's offer for more would be the only way to rescue the forgotten boy. These revelations demanded every ounce of faith and trust I had recently gained, and they also demanded an answer. Yet at the height of all this pressure and tension, a simple truth sprang from my heart—a truth which brought everything else into miraculous order. I wanted to be with Jesus.

I came to a point in my life and my faith where Christ was all that mattered—so much so that my life and my faith were not even relevant any longer. The lost boy was not relevant. My family was not relevant. And remarkably, God's offer of more was not relevant either. One thing was important. Everything else faded into the background as two central figures came into crystal clear view. In my prayer time one day an image pressed onto my spirit—Jesus and I standing face to face. The entire universe along with my whole existence seemed to be focused on this scene. The clarity of the image perfectly matched the clarity of what I needed to do. I told the Lord: "I don't care. I just want you."

I laid everything at his feet and threw my arms open to Him. I said yes to His offer, but there was a catch. My words were simple: "I want the 'more' you have for me because I want you, Lord." I only wanted Him. I did not care about anything else. An unquenchable thirst to know Him better and draw closer to Him filled my spirit. I had never experienced a stronger desire to love someone in my entire life. The sensation was all consuming. I felt confident that more would come, but I honestly could not focus on it. I wanted Jesus for who He was, not because of what He had done or what He now offered me. I counted the cost and leapt into His arms.

LEFT BEHIND

I know it sounded terrible to say I did not care about anything, but that was how I truly felt. Of course, I was not saying I had no concern for my family. I still loved and cared for them deeply, however, I knew that I could no longer put them or anything else before the Lord. I had already acknowledged that everything in my life was a blessing from Him. And now God helped me see that my family belonged to Him well before they belonged to me. Safe in this understanding, I felt His assurance that the best thing I could do for them was to seek Christ first.

As I grew more excited to continue seeking, reality came crashing back in. The toughest part of reality was a job which insisted on being a top priority. This company, along with all its upsides, wanted to own me. The running joke was that employees needed to buy the nicest house and priciest cars they could get. That way the company could be sure workers were selling hard to cover huge debt payments. Managers told me repeatedly that they wanted me to be heavily leveraged. While I tried to avoid that, I could not avoid being heavily engaged. I was now being asked to spend about twice as much time on the road, and the time away had already become a tremendous strain on the family. Time in general was a precious commodity during those days. In order to wedge some prayer and worship into my day, I was getting up at 5:00 A.M. Many nights I did not get to bed until after midnight. I was still serving at the church and trying to build my own Internet business. Basically I was busy. I was so busy in fact, I laughed out loud at the Lord one day when I sensed Him ask me to get alone with Him for three days of fasting and prayer. The idea of it sounded really great, but I knew that if I had three days to spare, I was going to spend it at home.

When I did get to be home, the pressure and stress of work made me tough to live with. Angela could once again tell I was unhappy, but this time she was much less tolerant. The trials of single parenting over the past several months had led to her own unhappiness. She wanted me home, but not for the purpose of adding to the tension in the house. I tried to help. I even tried to explain to her what I was going through spiritually, but since I could hardly explain it myself, I ended up making things worse. I seemed to give Angela the impression I wanted to be left alone. Even though that was not the case, I failed to see how I could bring her closer. Work had become such a grind, and so much friction developed between what I wanted to do and what I had to do, I could barely relate to the love of my life.

Things got worse when we found out we had our second miscarriage. I wanted to be there for Angela and mourn the loss together. But I was so busy, she pretty much had to go it alone. My heart ached for her. I wanted to give her support, physically, emotionally and spiritually. Yet I felt like I was falling down in all these areas, especially when it came to matters of the spirit. I had been praying for Angela fervently, and even praying with her when we could. And, in spite of this, we did not seem to connect on the spiritual level. We still counted our blessings and thanked God for what we had, but for me it had gone much deeper. Internally I had made the decision to forsake everything and follow Jesus at all costs. Angela was not at that place in her faith journey. While I did not expect her to be at that place, I hoped she would understand. I had to believe I was doing the right thing for her and the right thing for our family.

Chapter Fourteen

Coming Alive

"You will seek me and find me when you seek me with all your heart."

JEREMIAH 29:13

GOODBYE, FAREWELL...

"I think I made a mistake." I remember saying this to a close friend shortly after I started my job. When a person is making statements like that after only a month in, it should be a warning that something is wrong. I do not know what happened. It was only a few weeks earlier that I was standing in a huge auditorium with 5,000 of my co-workers during our annual sales kickoff. I remember thinking: *I can't believe I actually work for this company!* It seemed so cool.

At that time I was truly excited. How could you not be after experiencing something like that? I embraced the challenge of making a name for myself in a position that was new to the company. But things began to change when I realized that making a name for myself was the most important thing to my boss and to the company. I was told in no uncertain terms that I needed to take credit for as much as I could immediately. I do not fault my boss. He was under tremendous pressure to take a whole group of new people across thirteen states and make them perform right out of the gate. Many times I felt sorry for him because he seemed to be in a no-win situation. And I started to get the impression that I was in one as well. I strived harder and harder to rationalize my job, and things seemed to make less and less sense. Even though I hit my revenue targets, the perception was that I did not do enough to "drive" the sales that were coming in. Welcome to life in corporate America, right?

Yet the typical trials of corporate life did not explain everything. I was changing. My view of what was important had changed dramatically. I no longer sought validation from my job, my company or my performance. I was sickened by the thought of striving only for recognition. I said many times under my breath: "If I have to justify my position everyday, I should not be here." Something held me back from putting my nose to the grindstone. Sure, I could have worked harder, played the game. But my heart was not in it.

Mercifully, my boss realized my heart was not in it, and he sat me down before my one-year review. I will never forget the conversation. We talked openly about the fact that I was struggling. He said at this point he would have to put me on a performance improvement plan, but we agreed that it probably would not do any good if I did not want to be there. What he said next was one of the biggest gulps of pride I have ever had to swallow. He said: "Chris, I can see if I can get you a package." He meant a severance package. Fired. The word raced through my mind ripping up emotions as it traveled. My gut wrenched and my chest tightened to the point that I could barely breathe. I had never been fired from any job, not even the ones in high school. I had always been promoted and left on my own terms. At the most inopportune time, the reality of my situation and my emotions converged. I turned my head quickly to avoid my boss's stare as my eyes began to mist. In an instant, I was transported back to boyhood- to that vulnerable place God had recently revealed. I failed. I could not do it on my own. *Damn it!*

My boss was very gracious and understanding. He agreed it was a tough thing to accept, but he assured me that there was no shame in it. The paperwork went through as a "mutual termination," whatever that is, and on August 3, 2005 I left my second job in the span of a year-and-a-half.

THE BLANK PAGE

The craziest thing about this latest job fiasco is that it was actually one of the biggest blessings in my life. In spite of getting fired only a year after getting hired, I made more money than any previous year. Remember when I said it did not seem to matter that I hit my sales targets? The truth is I finished the year at a 130 percent of my objective. In addition, the severance package amounted to a half a year's salary paid out in a lump sum. Phil, my best friend and a strong brother in Christ, quickly reminded me that this must be a blessing and an opportunity from God. I was way ahead of him.

My thoughts had already shifted from wounded pride and a searing sense of failure to a profound longing and desire to seek the "more" God had promised. I felt free to respond to some of the requests He laid on my heart months earlier. I was ready. "I'm going to take some time," I told those close to me. "I'm not going to rush out and find a job right away." Even though most people looked at me like a dog stares at a TV, I did not care. God had been waiting patiently for a long time. It was time to let Him continue what He started.

One of the things He had initiated was a desire in my heart to journal my experiences. During a moment of particular spiritual clarity, I remembered the Lord's instruction from years earlier to "start writing." And now I felt I had at least a little more to say. Obediently, I cracked open a fresh new journal on the first day of my "extended vacation." It was August 4, 2005 and I wrote:

Angela told me today that she hasn't been happy in about a year-and-a-half.

It is the first day at home after being fired from my job. My own Internet business is struggling to get off the ground. My prayer time has been arduous at best. This sounds like the start of a great country song, though maybe not a great way to start a journal. I guess the upside is that future entries should be better. This is by no means a serious low point in my life. I am at a crossroads to be sure. I am mostly frustrated by the clash between uncertainty for the future and a divine sense of urgency. I feel like I'm blowing it—squandering opportunities as I've done so many times before.

I am so blessed. The Scripture: "…from the one who has been entrusted with much, much more will be asked" is running through my head (Luke 12:48). The deepening sense of those words tells me I'd better get on my horse. I've always felt that God has something great planned for me. I cried out for Him to show His will for me. I must follow it. I want to be the man He wants me to be. I want to love my wife better, love my kids better; be a better husband, dad, student, leader, friend, mentor and brother in Christ. Most importantly, I want to know Jesus better every day and walk with Him more closely. I have now committed to document that journey in the following pages.

Ok, it would seem I had a flare for the dramatic. Or maybe I had a sense that I might some day actually document my experience in a book someone might read. Either way, I was determined to let the Lord lead me where I needed to go.

Be With Me

One place I needed to go was away. When God put the request on my heart to seek Him in fasting and prayer, I laughed at Him. I was not laughing anymore. What seemed impossible to grant before was now as simple as picking the days. It was simple, but still not easy. Committing to three days alone with God was a tough assignment. I had no idea what to expect. I knew He had big things in store that were going to affect the rest of my life. It was one of those "be careful what you ask for" kinds of things. Nonetheless, my spirit told me it was time. So early in August, I planned a Thursday to Saturday stint at a friend's cabin on a lake about two hours north of town.

I awoke the morning of August 24 with a wide mix of feelings. Excitement and anticipation churned in my head along with anxiety and uncertainty. It was like getting ready for an adventurous trip or meeting up with a long lost friend—times ten. I found myself praying against expectation and preconceived notions. I genuinely wanted this to be about the Lord. I was doing this for Him. And yet it was impossible for my spirit to deny the sense that this would also be extremely beneficial for me.

I left at noon and drove north on M23. I drove in silence, trying to clear my thoughts and bring my heart, mind and spirit under the authority of Jesus Christ. I prayed that He would meet me there and that I would be open to His Word and the Holy Spirit. As if on cue, the spiritual attack began. I could feel the pull of the world, flesh and devil like a Great Dane yanking on my backside. "You shouldn't be doing this." "Angela is already frustrated with you. This will send her over the edge." "Nobody understands what you're doing. You look like a freak." "You don't even know what you're doing." "OK, smart guy, once you get there what are you going to do then?" This is only a small part of what went through my mind. The worst part was that I knew most of it was true. I had put this off for so long, and now that it was here, I did not know what to do. I know I did not want it to be three days of praying for the needs of everyone I knew and seeking answers to all of life's great questions. This was an obedience thing, an act of submission—a sacrifice. Granted, it was a small sacrifice compared to what Jesus did for me, but it was all I could offer at this point. Besides, the Lord had already begun to show me how being still before Him in worship is the source of life. I steadied my resolve by remembering that all blessings flow from this. I continued on, pulling into the dirt driveway of the small cabin at 3:00 P.M.

SHHHHHHH

I dumped my bag and some bottled water off in the cabin and went back outside to enjoy the warm Michigan afternoon sun. I found a wooden swing under a big shade tree and I settled in to read some Scripture. Still not being quite sure what to do, I figured reading the Bible was not a bad way to start. I asked the Lord to speak to me from these pages and I was lead to the Book of Daniel. Though I had read it before, it was like I was seeing it for the first time. I was not swept away in all of the prophecy, I was captured by the unwavering intimate faith he had in God. Though Daniel faced certain death a number of times, he knew that God would protect him. And he continued to give God the glory when he was placed in positions of authority. I thought: *Huh, giving God the glory in good times and bad. That just might work.* I realized how the examples from Scripture can be much more effective when we take the time to let them sink in.

While thanking God for this nugget of wisdom (as if it was the first time ever revealed), I noticed that my head was aching terribly. Wondering why that might be, I remembered that I had not eaten all day. Before I could even complete that thought, strong pangs of hunger joined in with my throbbing melon. Fasting is hard, especially when you are used to at least two cups of coffee a day. As I was beginning to dread the idea of another two days of this, the thought occurred to me: *You could pray for relief. Have a faith like Daniel's? It is worth a try,* I thought. I prayed simply, speaking the words out loud: "Lord, free me from this pain." The relief was instant. My headache was gone. The hunger pangs vanished. The change was so immediate and complete I could not believe it. I shook my head vigorously from side to side to make sure. I struggled to remember a time where God had answered a prayer so quickly. Still embroiled in disbelief, I felt the question of, "Why do you doubt Me?" settle on my spirit. Disbelief evaporated as the weight of the question filled me with reverence and humility. This pretty much set the tone for the rest of the time. I knew that the Lord was there.

In the same way my hunger and discomfort had lifted, all other distractions faded as well. Something clicked and I was placed squarely in the presence of Jesus. I took several walks in the woods and around the lake. All the while, I felt the Lord walking with me—peacefully, quietly—like an old friend who listens with unconditional love, saying little. He guided me through more of His Scripture, and the words came alive like never before. They seemed to leap off the page. I found myself singing the Psalms aloud and weeping at the power and depth of His teaching in the Gospels. A calming feeling enveloped my spirit as the Lord assured me I was on the right track. My countless blessings came into full view and my heart swelled with gratitude. Prayers began to flow easily, even conversationally, as I thanked God for my life, my wife and my children. I prayed passionately for Him to use me in helping others, especially those close to me, experience this same intimacy.

While praying this, I noticed heaviness join the calm in my spirit. It was clear that God was laying a large calling on my heart though He was not revealing the details. A familiar feeling of uncertainty mixed with excitement washed over me. I had experienced this many times throughout my life. But this time was different, better. Since the peace of the Lord was with me, I did not have the urge to ask, "What's going on?" or "What's this all about?" I knew somehow that God would reveal everything to me when the time was right. For now, He wanted me here. I sensed Him telling me "shhhh- hhh." At that moment, I began to see that this is what God truly wanted from me: to simply be with Him. And at that moment, I truly wanted nothing else.

LOST AND FOUND

On the last day of my time away, I asked the Lord to tell me if I had gone back and rescued the little boy as He instructed me to do. He reminded me of events that had taken place between the time he showed me this vision and the current day. I smiled as I recalled the fact that He had indeed taken me back, all the way back. Over the previous few months, I experienced a great deal of restoration and reconciliation. In the case with my mother, I discovered something on my heart that happened well before I had abandoned the boy. It happened even before I was born.

God led me to talk with my mom about my conception. I was conceived out of wedlock, but that topic was never discussed as I was growing up. It was not until my late teens that I went back and did the math myself. The fact that it had not been addressed left the question open in my mind: Was I truly wanted? This question affected me more deeply than I ever acknowledged. It led to the deeper questions that God had answered. Do I really matter? Am I worthy of being loved? Now, in His grace, the Lord was bringing those answers to fullness in my life.

As Mom and I talked, we experienced a tremendous healing time for both of us. It helped me connect to a larger story surrounding my life. I began to realize more fully how God can use any event, even one that seemed rooted in sin, for good. Though my parents had allowed their desire to overcome them, their genuine love for each other produced fruit that was pleasing to God. I thanked Him for this love and also for their love for me.

The Lord also led me to talk with Dad, mostly about his heart. It was a truly amazing exchange. Dad told me that he always saw himself doing something great. With tears in his eyes he said that maybe the something great was me. I was overcome by his words. I could sense the genuine pride and profound love in his voice. My heart ached with gratefulness. I thanked Dad for all he had done, and I told him that he was everything I needed a father to be. There were so many more things I wanted to say, but I could not find the words. I did say I loved him, and that was one thing we both knew we could always say. After Dad and I parted ways, I felt led to pray for his heart. It had soured a bit since the passing of his parents, and I prayed that he could not only feel my love but also feel the love of Jesus on his spirit. Lastly, I asked the Lord to help me honor that sense of greatness my father had shared.

As I reflected on these much needed and much appreciated conversations with my parents, the Lord impressed an image on my spirit. I saw the little boy and me walking hand in hand along a path. It was clear that neither of us was quite sure where we were going, but the boy had been found and now felt safe. It was like the old story of a grandpa walking with his grandson along a lonely country road. There was nothing but cornfields around for as far as the eye could see. After they walked for a while, the grandpa stopped and asked the boy, "Do you know where you are?" The child did not answer. As they walked on, the grandfather stopped again and asked the child, "Do you know where you are?" Again, the boy did not respond. A while later, having walked still further, the old man asked the boy a third time, "Now do you know where you are?" This time the grandson looked around and replied, "Sure, Grandpa, I'm walking with you." This image demonstrated the kind of faith God was asking of me. It was the kind of faith I had tried to demonstrate by following Him to this point. Peace and assurance swept over me as I realized the boy and I were on the right path. Even though our direction was unclear, we knew we were walking with God.

LESSONS

I prepared to leave the cabin and found that I had a few more minutes before I needed to officially end my time away. My heart was filled with mixed emotions. I did not want to leave, but felt so rejuvenated and alive that I could not stay put. In an effort to squeeze every last drop of life from this time, I sat quietly on my knees and reflected on the amazing things Jesus had shown me during these few days. He had lovingly and graciously reminded me of the power of prayer. He bolstered my desire for discipline and obedience through a truly joyous time of fasting. And He brought His Holy Word to life, giving me an intense hunger for Scripture. With all these tremendous blessings still in mind, I asked Him to direct me once again to a place in the Bible so I could spend a few more precious moments in His Word. The Lord replied with: "Thessalonians, First Thessalonians." The clarification made me chuckle, because He knew that my response would be: "Oh, right, there's more than one." With my lack of Bible knowledge in tow, I fumbled around until I found the book. I received the words as great instruction on how to live a life of love for others and how to walk in the assurance of Christ. Nothing in particular jumped out at me except for Chapter 4, verse 11: "Make it your ambition to lead a quiet life…" (1 Thessalonians 4:11). This part of the verse struck a chord in my spirit which brought the whole three days into focus.

Evidently, this time of fasting and prayer was not to be an isolated event. I became fully aware that in recent years, I had not made it my ambition to lead a quiet life. Yet now that I had begun to quiet myself, I needed to take forward what I had learned in these last few days. God had revealed that the key to a quiet life was a quiet heart and a quiet spirit. He impressed upon me that the time ahead would require a significant commitment and desire to remain still before Him. I thanked Him for fostering that level of commitment and desire in me, and as I did, my gratitude overflowed into a tidal wave of humility. I knew it would not be easy to continue this journey with Christ, and I suddenly felt vulnerable and inadequate. My faith seemed so small. I understood that there was so much I still did not know. There were so many questions that did not have answers. I cried out to God in total reliance on Him, saying: "I can't do this without you."

Instantly, His grace descended upon me. I was once again filled with promise. I believed that everything would unfold according to His timing and will. The knowledge illuminated my soul that having all the answers right now was not the point. Drawing closer to Christ and building my faith in Him was the goal. I knew that doing this would put me in line to receive the answers and so much more. As I got in the car, my energy and excitement were at their peak. My spirit seemed to be buzzing with the work of the Lord's will in my life. Things beyond my vision and my control were definitely in motion. I felt like I could take on the world. Little did I know I would be doing that very thing.

Chapter Fifteen

In the Presence

"Be still, and know that I am God . . ."

PSALM 46:10

OPPOSED

It did not take long for the world to kill my spiritual buzz. My car broke down on the way home from the cabin. I managed to get it restarted and limp back to the family. Angela was glad to see me, but she was obviously frustrated with the kids and with the current state of affairs. I could feel the negativity surrounding her and them. In the weeks that followed, life grew even more stressful around the house. As one could expect, Angela wondered why I was not working. She would definitely have liked me to be employed or at least be seeking employment as quickly as possible. Being fully aware of this, I felt a large amount of guilt and shame set in, especially whenever Angela brought up the topic. She felt I was just being selfish, even though I was not. I was trying to be the absolute opposite of selfish by submitting to God wholly and completely, and allowing Him to speak His instruction to my heart.

In many ways Angela understood this, and she was deeply appreciative of my commitment to grow in Christ. Yet at the same time she felt like she was losing me. On a few occasions she lamented that she wanted the fun me back. Even though I was around the house, I often seemed to be emotionally and mentally checked out. In her mind, virtually nothing had changed from when I was traveling all the time. She confessed to me sometime later that it looked as though I was having an affair. I could certainly understand why she felt that way.

God had not given me any instruction on how to relate to those I left behind in my quest to follow Him with reckless abandon. Maybe that is why it is called reckless. I tried to love my wife and kids the best I could, but I had long ceased going to them for validation. That could very well have been the biggest change. I was now receiving validation from Jesus and Angela felt like she had been left holding the bag. On top of that, her security was threatened as it had been during my last job change. I tried to do much of the same things to help around the house as I did before, but this time she gave me a much different response. I think she felt such a loss of control she recoiled against my encroachment on her duties and responsibilities. She took it upon herself to sequester the kids and give me space even though I was not asking for it. I tried to honor her by staying out of her routine, but I also felt responsible for disrupting her world and stealing the love of her life.

In addition to these obvious family pressures, I knew the forces of darkness would be against me, so I tried to prepare myself. With the assurance God had given me, I was confident I had nothing to fear. Yet, when a distinct sense of fear did set in during this time, I began to grow confounded and a little concerned. I asked the Lord to help me understand what was making me so afraid. I also took my concerns and feelings to Phil, who had now become my closest friend and accountability partner. We both came to understand that fear was merely a symptom, or a manifestation of a bigger root issue in my life. So in my prayer time, I asked the Lord to let me see where that fear came from, and on what it was based. I asked Him to take me there. I submitted to God, seeking His presence, and pressing into Him, saying: "Lord, I want to go there because I want to be wholehearted in You."

Still I knew that getting there might not be that simple. The usual mind monsters were working overtime this morning. Many thoughts of things I needed to do and things I had not done were pounding on my head. On top of that, I faced numerous external distractions. Chiming doorbells and ringing phones seemed to be perfectly timed to destroy any and all intimacy. Yet I stood fast and I stayed committed. The Lord took me through Psalms 27 and 51. "Be still and wait on the LORD" (Psalm 27:14) clung to my heart as I remained patient and continued to press in. I refused to let the distractions pull me away from what I knew I needed to do. I began praising and worshipping Him. After reading the Psalms and meditating on them, I began to sing out loud. I started singing: "Let it rain, open the flood gates of Heaven." I repeated the line, singing as if I were in church. I let the words flow from my heart. I sang loudly, then softly, then loud again. And slowly, slowly but surely, the Lord met me there.

THE WALL

As Jesus enveloped me in His presence, He revealed to me what was behind the wall of fear: Pain. At that moment, I remembered this connection of fear and pain from several months earlier. During an extended prayer time at a church I was visiting, God showed me a brief glimpse of this intense pain. I took it to be the pain He feels when I shrink back from being the man He wants me to be. When I cowered in fear and refused to step up, it grieved His heart terribly. The weight of this on my heart was excruciating and unbearable. I told the Lord I never wanted to feel that pain again. It was too immense. I could not handle it. In an effort to avoid it, I made a vow to not grieve Him by shrinking back ever again. I was very thankful for what the Lord showed me that day. I viewed it as a great victory. But now in His presence this morning, I realized I might have misinterpreted those events from the past.

I started to understand that the pain I felt that day was not only what He feels for me, but also the pain that had not been released from my old wounds. And, sure enough, what I did when I said I never wanted to feel that pain again was make an agreement. However, it was not an agreement with God; it was an agreement with the devil. It was an agreement to "not go there" and to bottle up that pain. This was a practice I had perfected since childhood. I had built a huge wall around the pain over the years and decades because I was petrified to feel it. Each time I refused to go there, I threw another stone of fear on the wall. And now I stood squarely before it. I realized that in order to move toward Jesus, the wall had to come down. Of course I did not want to deal with the pain behind the wall, and by this time the fear was so paralyzing, I could not force myself to breakthrough. The only thing that saved me was my desire for the Lord. I would have been frozen in this fearful purgatory had I not remembered why I was here in the first place. This was not a journey to find inner healing. I was not even asking to be freed from this frightful existence. I had come seeking Him and Him alone. If through that wall was the only way to get to Jesus, then the wall was most certainly coming down.

The second I acknowledged this with my spirit, the wall exploded and Christ began to address the pain. The experience was difficult to fathom. I had been standing while I praised and worshipped Him, and as Christ dealt with the pain, He brought me to my knees, literally. The pain was so intense I could not hold my own weight. I collapsed in a heap on the floor sobbing loudly.

This went on to the point that I noticed my nose had begun to run profusely. In a bazaar moment of worlds colliding, I mustered the strength to get a tissue while remaining fully in the presence of the Lord Almighty. I was totally controlled by His powerful grasp. I knew that nothing in Heaven or on earth could have severed the conduit of healing. And as He continued to remove the pain, I kept on sobbing and blubbering. My chest heaved as I took in huge gulps of air. My body wrenched and convulsed as I cried harder than I had ever cried before. I cried longer than I had ever cried before. I did not even bother trying to stop, because I knew I would not be done until Jesus was done. I felt my heart being emptied as if someone had flushed a big pain toilet. It seemed to take years, but slowly the hurt began to subside and my sobs reduced to quiet weeping. In the relative calm, I noticed that there was now a huge vacancy in my heart.

FILLING UP

As soon as I noticed this vacancy, I felt the onset of a new sensation. My heart shook violently under the strain of being refilled. I could tell instantly what was happening. I was being filled with the Holy Spirit. The weight of His fullness was so overwhelming I could do nothing else but cry out to God, "OK, OK, OK." As a child submitting to his father in learning to swim or ride a bike, I gave up control. He had complete and total access to my heart and spirit at that moment. I had no ability to hold anything back. Everything He did was met with total acceptance. It was a remarkable healing sensation. I kept repeating the phrases over and over: "OK, OK" and "I will, I will."

As this sense of being filled continued to wash over me, I began to realize the reason for my repeated statements. I was making an agreement with God. I was not even sure what I was agreeing to, but it did not matter. I could sense a vast download of knowledge flowing into my spirit. God was speaking directly to it. Though I could not hear the words audibly or discern their meaning in my mind, I could tell there were many things imparted to me—things I was certain would be revealed to me fully at a later date.

The feeling was so immense and powerful; I could not break free from the crying or the agreeing. Nor did I want to. I sat on my knees rocking back and forth, letting His love fill me up and letting His power crash over me in wave after wave. The acknowledgment went on for what could have been hours, though likely it was only a few minutes. I had lost all sense of time. The only thing I could sense was the shifting taking place in my spirit. This shift was from pain and anguish to joy and elation; pure elation and joy unspeakable. I had never experienced anything like it.

At that moment, my sobbing turned from cries of sorrow to boisterous laughter. It was uncontrollable and it bordered on hysterics. I experienced high-pitched laughing, low, full belly roaring and everything in between. This kept on to the point that I began to ask in my own mind: "What am I doing?" I could hear myself laughing and it seemed so foolish. Yet, right then, I did not care because I was so caught up in the Holy Spirit. His glory and joy showing about me and flowing in me became so great I could do nothing but laugh and shake on the floor.

After a time, I attempted to get back on my knees to pray, but I immediately collapsed and fell against the wall. I found myself wedged against the bed and a box of copy paper in our spare bedroom/office. I could not move! I had no power or desire to move so I simply lay there suspended in the Lord's joy and in the joy He had released to me. I basked in the fullness of the Holy Spirit, continuing to laugh and continuing to say: "OK, Lord, OK."

Then suddenly I was back on my feet. The Lord had lifted me off my back before I realized I had even moved. I began to thank Him over and over. I praised and worshipped His name. I gushed with gratitude over what He had done. I kept on saying, "OK, I will," in the full knowledge that there was so much more to be revealed. I knew for a fact He would reveal it according to His good pleasure.

A wonderful sense of peace settled on my spirit. I felt so thankful that He gave me the strength, courage and desire to press into Him, and to fight through the opposition. Coming through on the other side of the pain felt like an astounding accomplishment. It was one of the hardest things I had ever done. This had been the most difficult journey of my life to this point, but it was worth it. I could now feel the presence of God and the presence of the Holy Spirit working in me and filling me up in a way I never knew was possible.

Clean and New

After breaking through and being filled up with the Holy Spirit, I noticed a distinct difference in my faith walk. While there were still times where I had to fight through distraction and press into the Lord, I was now experiencing something else. I could discern the Holy Spirit pressing in on me. One such event happened a few weeks later as I was lying in bed, struggling to fall asleep. I could sense the welcome heaviness of something coming, but I did not give it much thought at the time. I had no clue I was headed for an amazing and wonderful revelation from God.

Instead, my thoughts were swirling around a growing concern on my heart. I had been concerned lately about the power of God manifesting itself in my life. It may seem funny to say that, considering the amount of time and effort I had put into seeking Him. But now that it was starting to "show" itself, I was apprehensive about the effect it was having on other people. I was beginning to hear positive words from others about how my actions and behaviors were touching them. I consistently tried to assure them that it was not me, but Jesus who was "touching" them. And He was simply using me as His vessel. At the same time, those positive words made me feel really good. I found myself getting worried about "using" the power God had given me to satisfy my ego instead of glorifying Him. It was obvious that the power of the Holy Spirit had been misused and abused by many, seeking validation from men without giving the honor and praise back to God. I was terrified that I might become one of the many. As my anxiety grew, I began to sense that this feeling might be the reason for the Lord's pressure on me. The following morning, I felt the Holy Spirit continue to press on my spirit. I knew I was going to have to bring it before God. Through prayer and worship I pressed in to meet Him, and He quickly brought me into a vision standing before Jesus. My songs of worship faded into tears as Jesus allowed me to fall at His feet and clutch His robe. His beauty and light began to overwhelm me. As I sat up, I could see His face coming closer to me and I could feel His hands on me. He brought His face so close to mine that I felt his hair brush my cheek. Indescribable love and warmth coursed through my entire body. I reached out to touch His hair, as if to make sure it was really what I had felt. At that moment, I knew I must be laid bare before Him. A tremendous desire to be uncovered before Christ welled up in my heart as I consented with my spirit. In an instant I found myself completely naked, sprawled before Jesus on an altar, as a lamb prepared for sacrifice. Then I noticed a blinding white light shining in front of me. It was so pure and clean. Words could not describe its depth and beauty. In a strange manner, the light was apart from Jesus, but it also emanated from Him. There was no question that this was the Glory of God. As my eyes sat fixed on the Light, I noticed in my periphery that Jesus had knelt next to me. He placed His hand inside my chest and cupped my heart. I felt the deepest cleansing and renewal I had ever experienced. No part of me was in darkness. Every corner of my being was brought into full view of the intense, penetrating Light. There was so much love and intimacy I could not grasp it all.

Physically, my body was a wreck. I sat slumped over in a chair, crying uncontrollably. Stuff poured from every opening on my face. I was groaning and straining under the intense pressure on my heart. I could feel my entire body twisting and tightening around my chest. I cried out over and over, "My God, my God." I sensed no pain, but I did sense the incredible weight of powerful hands resting on me. As Jesus completed His work on my heart, He stood. I lay there, continuing to sob and weep softly. At that moment, my cell phone rang right in front of me and startled me out of my vision.

THE ROBE

Completely out of my wits, I took the phone call and cleaned myself up. Even thought I was seemingly ripped from this intimate time prematurely, I knew that I still remained in Christ's presence. I got on my knees and picked up the vision again with great ease. With the Light still shining in front of us, I was helped to my feet by Jesus and the Holy Spirit. I felt completely washed anew. My spirit was fresh and my heart was light, although I still felt powerful hands resting on me. I began to thank the Holy Spirit profusely. I was so grateful to Him for gently prodding me and leading the way to this point. I stood with Jesus on my left side and the Holy Spirit on my right. While we stood, a question of, "OK, what now?" came to me. As I pondered the silliness of the question I noticed that they were looking at me, and I was staring lovingly into the Light. Then Jesus asked the obvious question, "Would you like to go there?" As I ran through my mind things like "Uh, yeah, you bet, shuh," the only response I could muster was, "Yes, Lord." No sooner did I utter the phrase than I looked down and realized I was still naked. Well, in my newfound wisdom, I understood that I could not go there looking like this. So I turned my eyes to Jesus as if to ask what I needed to do. Then He asked: "Would you like your anointing?" Again I responded, "Yes, Lord". But this time I was not as sure of myself. All of the things I had been struggling with came flooding back to me. What if I messed up? What if I abused the power? What if I got caught up in people praising me? In response, Jesus motioned for me to look over my right shoulder as He said: "Worry and concern are still there. You can go back with them if you like." It was a kind offer, but thankfully I refused. Instead,

I looked to Jesus and said, "No, Lord, I am Your servant. I desire what You have for me." With that, Jesus and the Holy Spirit placed a robe of pure white over my head. As they did, that same intense feeling of love and warmth covered my entire body. Once again, I was overwhelmed in the physical. Sobs and laughter came pouring out simultaneously as I shook and rocked on my knees. The robe was so brilliant in its purity and cleanness. I stood in awe as it flowed over my arms, over my shoulders and chest and down to the floor. I could hardly contain myself as I tried to take in its beauty and brightness. The robe seemed to glow with a light of its own. Similar to the Light in Jesus, it seemed to be connected to, yet distinct from the Light of God's Glory. I felt completely validated and totally unworthy at the same time. Unsure of the future and my own ability, I stood ready to walk on with Jesus leading the way. He assured me that the full knowledge of my anointing would be revealed as the mysteries of God's Kingdom unfolded. I was excited for the next part of this journey to begin.

GLORY

With all I had seen and experienced in such a short time, it was hard to believe that anyone would be expecting more. Yet I knew God had much more in store for me; and I knew that the best way to find it was to keep my focus on Him. I was now hearing the voice of God regularly and experiencing His presence on a consistent basis. Though my time alone with the Lord was still a struggle against, well, everything, I felt a constant connection that seemed to be unbreakable. And as I continued to seek Christ, the connection only got stronger.

About two weeks after the New Year, I received a word from the Lord regarding the path that lay before me. I saw myself once again; standing in the place where Jesus and the Holy Spirit were waiting for me to journey on with them. In this continuation of the vision, a larger path began to appear at my feet. It was illuminated by God's glory, by the robe of my anointing, and also by the Light of Christ and the Holy Spirit. As it cut through the darkness, I noticed the path leading off in a direction not directly toward God. Yet I knew it was of Him. During this time in my life, I had been questioning so much, but in spite of my uncertainty, God's grace and wisdom brought many things to me. The first thing He revealed was that the path ahead is not "safe." Immediately following this He said I should avoid being enticed or seduced by the abundance that would come. I understood this to mean that the future had much to unfold: great trials and struggles and also tremendous provision, abundance and joy. I welcomed it. I welcomed the Lord, and all He had for me.

On the heels of this extended vision, I felt significant unrest. I am not sure if it was a test or a direct spiritual attack, but my mind abruptly shifted back to the situation at home. I was still not getting along with Angela. She was very upset with me regarding our financial situation and with the fact that I was still not working. She wanted to know what was next. She watched patiently as the money we had set aside drained away day by day. In contrast, I focused only on the assurance that this was God's provision and we were under His care. I wished I could have been more comforting to her, but I did not know what to say. In all honesty, the uncertainty was weighing heavily on me as well. This time had taken its toll on our marriage and our family, but I knew it was totally worth it. I prayed, as I had many times before, for Angela to be comforted and reassured. I understood that God could say and more and do more for her during this time than I ever could.

Returning to my time with the Lord, I asked Him to open up His Word to me. He took me to Isaiah 42:10-17. As I read and got down to verse 16, it suddenly hit me that what the Lord was speaking to me was truly His voice. Verse 16 says:

I will lead the blind by ways they have not known. Along unfamiliar paths I will guide them. I will turn the darkness into light before them and make the rough places smooth. These are the things I will do. I will not forsake them.

The second I read it, I completely broke down. The Lord's Light burst into the room and instantly ceased my body, mind and spirit. His Glory obliterated me. I began sobbing yet again. But this time the sobs were of immense joy. The crying turned quickly into uncontrollable laughter—

once more to the point of hysteria. Yet this was no emotional experience. It was without a doubt the presence of God—His manifest presence over me. I felt the power of the Holy Spirit more strongly than I ever had. I had very little feeling in my body. I was fully aware in my mind, but my heart and spirit were so overjoyed, uplifted and heightened, it was as if I was not even in my body. I am not referring to the clichéd, "out of body experience." It was simply an intense focus on the Glory of God. All I could do was stare straight up. My view was filled with the blinding Light of this Glory. The beauty and power of it was beyond comprehension. Its depth and purity were immeasurable. It kept me transfixed for what had to be an hour or more. I lay there with my arms stretched upward, worshipping God. It was the purest and truest worship experience I could imagine.

Tears continued to stream from my eyes. They were tears of abundant joy and delight. I was in disbelief and total awe of how beautiful He was. I could not move. I was frozen in His presence. I would never forget how wonderful it was for Him to suspend me in His Glory for that long. I basked in Him. I praised Him. I brought many prayers and requests for all the people in my life to Him. I prayed and pleaded with the Lord again and again to help me show this to others. I wanted to share the experience so they could know it was not some silly emotional high, or something that only happened in a big church worship frenzy. It was a true intimate, deep, loving, focusing, cleansing connection with God. I knew it was available for all of His children. I thanked Him for revealing His word to me along with His glory and for providing a peace that truly transcends all understanding.

Chapter Sixteen

Journey On

You have made known to me the paths of life; you
will fill me with joy in your presence."

Acts 2:28

Learning to Walk

As my journey continued, I came to realize that God wanted to bring up more things from the past that were less than pleasant. I felt my spirit spinning up to the point that I thought I was under a spiritual attack. I figured it was Ol' Scratch trying to trip me up once again. Yet I did not feel compelled to come against it because my "praydar" was not going off in the usual manner. It was weird. If it was truly an attack, I felt fairly sure I would have sensed it by this point in my walk. Since I had little clarity, I let the feeling drift into the background but did not completely dismiss it. The things from the past I am referring to were images of times I had hurt people or times when I had messed up pretty dramatically. As one might expect, there was quite a repertoire of these occurrences to pull from. They popped up periodically over a two-week span, and after a while they became quite annoying. I started having dreams depicting people in my life berating me because I had messed up, or was blowing it somehow.

Finally, the next morning, I felt it coming. I knew I would get some quality time with the Lord, so I began preparing myself. I expected a fight.

Sure enough, it was a battle. I could not clear my thoughts. My mind was spinning so fast I could not still my spirit. As I strained and struggled to calm myself and break through, a very graphic analogy came to my mind: spiritual constipation. I needed relief in a big way, but I could not figure out what was holding me back. Out of sheer exasperation, I resorted to doing something I knew how to do. I began to pray an intercessory prayer. I started by praying for a boy we had recently sponsored in Africa. I prayed for him and his family. I poured out my heart. I prayed honestly and fervently that he could know Jesus and feel His love. For whatever reason, that opened the door. God began to let me feel the weight of His anointing and a glimpse of the power He wants to release in my life. I was dumfounded. I felt totally unworthy, unprepared and confused. Since this latest spin-up had been all about my failures, mistakes and inadequacies, I questioned how I was going to carry out His plan. Then the Lord revealed that what I had been experiencing was not an evil attack, but conviction on my spirit as part of the training I was receiving. He went on to say that I still carried fear, fear of letting Him down. I was petrified of messing up the plan He had for me. I realized I had to let my past track record go and accept that I was still going to mess up. In fact, He bluntly stated that: "If I'm going to use you on a grand scale, you must be willing to mess up on a grand scale. Move forward anyway."

The Lord continued with still more instruction on how I was to move forward. He told me I must learn to walk with Him instead of running back and forth to Him. I should also resist the urge to leave Him behind and rush into battle. I understood that it was not enough to fight for my King, I had to fight with Him as well. The urge to go it alone had grown out of my childhood need to prove my maturity. To overcome this, I began praying against the spirits of independence, self-reliance and self sufficiency. God revealed these things to be rooted in pride, arrogance and vanity. I needed to learn to be interdependent, always reliant upon the Lord. He went on to show me that I still struggled with extending kindness and compassion, and this struggle came from a remaining need to be validated. In my effort to prove myself or my point, I could be hurtful and harsh in my attitude, words and actions. The Lord reminded me that humility came from obedience, and that only by continuing to walk in His Spirit could I have the proper balance of authority and modesty. Lastly, He spoke these amazing words to my spirit:

> Prudence and expediency will be crucial for your walk. Your insatiable desire to run and tell the world is a gift I have given you. But it is a pitfall when you use it to gain validation from men. My anointing goes before you. The time has come, My son, to move as I move. You were made for such a time as this. Do not be afraid that you will let Me down. That feeling does not come from Me, and you know it. Guard your heart, but do not fear. You must leave fear behind for good. It has no place in My plan for you. Enjoy this time, My son. Draw from its richness. Abide in Me.

HE TOILS

The knowledge that many of my struggles were rooted in sin did not shock me. I was well aware of my continuing propensity for sin and the three pillars of anger, lust and fear still had a stronghold in my life. I truly repented from these sins, and I accepted the victory Christ had given, yet I still had difficulty walking in that victory. In an effort to gain a deeper understanding, I cried out to the Lord. He revealed to me that I was dealing not only with my individual sin but generational sin as well. I also realized that bringing sin before Him and letting it go were two different things. During this prayer time, I yielded to God as never before, and I experienced a shift in the attitude of my heart when praying for forgiveness and freedom. When I prayed before, it was usually to say: "Lord, help me fight this," or "Lord, give me strength to turn away." Now I was approaching Him as a child, asking Him not to help me or give me strength, but for Him to just take it. In the full knowledge that there was nothing I could do, I gave my struggle with sin over to Christ, as a helpless boy calls out to his father in a panic. In the blink of an eye, a vision came before me. I saw myself standing yet completely entangled in a mass of thick vines. They were wrapped around my midsection, extending off behind me. I was straining with all my might to tear free from the massive, gnarled limbs, but to no avail. It was obvious that I was hopelessly trapped and unable to move.

Standing there beside me over my right shoulder was Jesus. He looked as one expects Him to look; flawless, perfect, beautiful, and powerful. His gaze was soft but piercing. His robe was a flowing, spotless white garment, fitting for the King. He said nothing, but in His right hand He held a massive, shinning steel blade. It was like an oversized machete, or a threshing sickle. He stood perfectly still, looking not at my person in the vision, but directly at me. The steel blade glimmered in the bright sunlight. Jesus was waiting, waiting for something.

Suddenly, I realized that He was waiting for my heart! This image was a result of the attitude in my heart changing to one of total reliance on Him. The split second I acknowledged this, the Lord went to work. His total focus was on severing the vines. He attacked the thicket with such a brutal vengeance, my entire soul shook in reverent fear. I could feel the immense power of His righteous anger as He began to toil against the massive overgrowth entangling me.

I stood there wincing as Jesus grunted with each blow. The blade sank deeper and deeper into the vines as they cracked and splintered. Huge chards of wood flew off in every direction. It would have been an impressive show of force for even the largest man-made machine. I could only look on in helpless disbelief as the Lord's pure white robe became soiled with dirt and ripped by the snarl of thorns and jagged wood. His hands and arms were repeatedly scratched and gouged to the point that blood flowed heavily and flew off in droplets as He continued to swing harder and harder.

The Lord worked tirelessly, not once pausing to wipe the sweat streaming off his brow. The intensity of the vision was overwhelming. I began weeping violently. Everything inside me desired to cry out at once: "No, Lord! Let me do it. You've done so much already!" But I knew that was exactly what I could not do. As much as it hurt to see the Lord toil for my sin, it was what I had to allow if I have any hope of gaining the victory that He desired for me. I threw control over to Christ fully and completely. It was the only way. By His grace, I remained silent and allowed Him to finish his work. After quite a while, Jesus ceased hacking and straightened Himself with a deep cleansing breath. The sigh expressed His satisfaction over a job well done. I sensed a huge release on my heart and spirit. God's confidence and power washed over me. I felt completely liberated from the clutches of darkness.

Many times I told God I could not do this alone and that I needed His help. Yet it was another thing entirely to watch Him do all the work. The story of the Cross, at times, seemed so huge and so impersonal to me. Christ died for all the world's sins. How could I get my head around that? I knew it was amazing and beautiful. It was the greatest show of unconditional love the world has ever witnessed. But it also meant that this price was paid for my individual sins every time I brought them to Him. As I said, it was the only way. Christ was the only way. The biggest obstacle for me was having the courage to lay down control and let Jesus endure my personal sins and work to free me from bondage. I thanked the Lord for doing what I could not do. I thanked Him for working so hard to free me.

FORGIVE ME

Allowing the Lord to deal with my sin was an obvious need I had to face. Having the Lord help me deal with myself in the aftermath was not so obvious. In the wake of His work on my sins another concern surfaced: self hatred. I did not know it was a root issue. I knew I had issues with feeling unworthy, and I thought those were resolved when I accepted the fact that I truly mattered to God. I believed Him when He told me. I had also turned away from calling myself an idiot. Yet I did not realize until a subsequent morning prayer time how deeply rooted this was. I assumed that having God provide my validation and recovering the wounded little boy were enough to make me wholehearted. Still, after all I had learned, something continued to hold me back. I prayed and meditated on this for months. I cried out to the Lord, asking for an answer. I accepted no answer many times. This morning, alone again in another hotel room, I was determined to simply receive and believe. That phrase repeated in my head as I worshipped, praised and pressed in. I felt the presence of the Holy Spirit coming on me. I sensed a closeness on my spirit more strongly than I had in a long time. As if it had never happened before, I felt very uneasy and unprepared. I heard a voice in the back of my mind say: "Not now, Lord. I've got to get into the shower in a few minutes." I could have easily stayed with that thought and gone on with my day. But this time I chose to stay. I continued to press in. I fought back the world and the flesh.

Surely the Lord's presence descended upon me. As I felt Jesus by my side, another vision formed before me. It was a soft yet intense white light which mixed to a blue color as it extended further and further out from its center into the surrounding darkness. I had seen this before. It was the Glory of God, the throne room, the Holy of Holies. I had basked in this when I was transfixed but had also seen it on the path. We were closer now. The light almost looked to be a portal or a narrow passage. It was extremely inviting, yet it looked to be a very tight fit. I sensed Jesus affirm me as I asked the question: "You mean I can go there?" His words came back softly and lovingly: "Yes, but not without a whole heart." Before I could start to ponder what that meant, I looked over my shoulder to see a person that appeared to be me being pulled by his arms to where I was standing. This image of me was striking. My heels were dug in to the ground and I was yanking back with all my might, yelling "No, no!" As I watched this unsettling picture of me, I felt my spirit ask: "What am I doing?" This other me was pulled right up before me. As we stood face to face, I looked to Jesus wondering what I should do now. He simply said: "Talk to him." In obedience I asked what was wrong. "Why don't you want to go there?" I said. "Because I don't trust you" was my response. "Why don't you trust me?" I asked. "Because you hate me," I replied.

At that second, all of the times I had torn myself down, called myself and idiot and belittled myself came flooding back A rush of sadness and remorse washed over me. The words "I'm sorry" sprang from my lips over and over again. "Please forgive me." I pleaded as the years of abusing myself and severe unkindness flashed before me. "I don't know. It has been so long," came the reply. Clearly this would take time to overcome. This leftover, stuffed down, broken remainder of me, which was still mired in the flesh, would need some time to forgive.

Realizing this, I immediately pointed to Jesus and said: "He can help you. He loves you more than you know. Don't you believe that?" "I want to," this other me responded. The entire event seemed so bazaar. This part of me wanted to trust God, but it was terribly afraid of being betrayed. I blamed it every time I sinned or fell short. I condemned this dark part of my heart for relying on all it had ever known; the world and the flesh. As the shock of the vision and conversation set in, the task ahead of me became clear. I needed to learn how to deny my sins without hating that part of me that wanted to cling to them. As strange as it sounded, I had to love myself fully and accept my own apology if I was to be truly wholehearted before the Lord. I knew it was critical to the next part of my journey.

It took nearly a month, but finally, I forgave myself, out loud, with my words and with my heart. Before I could do this, the forgotten me had to cry out to Jesus, confess his love, ask for forgiveness and believe in Him. With Christ by my side and with the strength of the Holy Spirit, I led my broken heart to freedom; just as one might lead a friend to salvation. The experience was hard to describe. I felt relief and victory, release, wholeheartedness and peace. I could tell a door had been opened and a new time was beginning. I praised God for His patience and goodness. I thanked Him for showing me the vision and for His unending love and compassion, and I marveled at the level of caring He showed in bringing me to and through this time.

New Season

With all the activity happening in my spiritual life, it would be easy to assume I had completely checked out of my physical life. While to many this may have appeared to be exactly the case, in truth, I was more plugged into my life now than I ever had been. I grew painfully aware of my blessings. The richness and depth of my relationships overwhelmed me. I could not believe how God had honored me, and I sought to honor Him by loving people the way He loved me.

The obvious place to start was my marriage. This time had been a tremendous challenge for Angela and me. She had been amazingly supportive while struggling to overcome uncertainty and her own issues with security. We argued and disagreed frequently over the situation. She continued to call me lazy and selfish and I told her I did not need to defend my actions to her. We both knew this was not a healthy way to air our grievances, but at least they got aired. Through the course of several tough discussions, we realized we were not fighting each other, we were fighting together. This sparked a renewed commitment to bring Christ into our marriage. We began praying together and asking for His Grace and strength as a couple. We prayed for our children and for our concerns side by side. We talked more openly and forgave one another for our harsh words. Ultimately, our faith in the Lord and respect for each other brought us closer. His peace enveloped our house and our marriage. We knew God would carry us through the times of uncertainty and bring new opportunities according to His plan.

As the spring thaw moved into Michigan, God began revealing some of these new opportunities. I found a job that would allow me to work from home and travel moderately. It was for much less money, but it came with much less stress. It seemed like an ideal fit for our lifestyle, and after seven months of living with little income, it was an ideal fit for our bank account. It was definitely an answer to prayer. Another answer to prayer came in an unexpected way. One day while riding in the car, my daughter told Angela she wanted a baby sister. Angela playfully responded by saying she should pray to God and ask Him for that. A short time later, we found out that the Lord had granted Gianna's prayer. In March we discovered we were going to have our fourth child, and later that fall, Isabella arrived to even out the kids at two boys and two girls.

I felt so grateful to share in these wonderful blessings with Angela and the kids. Still there were things happening on my spirit which I struggled to show them. I yearned to share all my experiences, but I really did not want to freak anyone out. Fortunately, the Lord had blessed me with a tremendous friend in Phil. As we talked more and more, we realized that God was moving in our lives in much the same way. Phil started down this crazy path to intimacy with Christ before I had, so as I mentioned, he became a wonderful mentor in the early days. As time moved on, we realized that we were quickly becoming peers and our friendship grew into an amazing brotherhood of trust and unconditional love. We shared our experiences openly and spoke wisdom and grace into each others lives. We prayed for one another fervently and discovered a brotherly love that neither of us knew existed. Phil's friendship provided a critical link between what was happening in my spirit and what was going on in my life. I thanked God for such an amazing friendship and family, and I looked forward to how He would use me in further honoring His astounding gifts.

SHARE YOUR STORY

"Tell your story. Share your story." The words were soft and low during yet another amazing time alone with the Father. As His words settled on my spirit, I experienced a wide array of emotions: fear, joy, pain and relief mixed in with excitement, sadness, thankfulness and humility. God's generosity pressed in on me yet again as affirmation filled me from head to toe. These were words I desperately needed to hear even though I had received many like them previously. I knew this was my calling. Wisdom and revelation imparted to my spirit had made it clear. Hours of prayer, meditation and study of Scripture confirmed it. And if that was not enough, many of those close to me felt that this was what I should do as well. But in spite of all this, I was not feeling much passion or commitment to follow through. I had been reviewing the pages of my journal in an effort to figure out what was holding me back. To avoid being disobedient, I asked God to show me if there was an issue. With stern yet loving words He responded:

Write the book. It is time to step out of your own way. Let me do My work in you. Stop filtering. Stop arguing with yourself over what I am telling you. It disrupts the work of the Holy Spirit. Your mind is being renewed. Allow it to come in line with your inmost being. Chastising your mind because it continues to question hinders the process. Find glory in the mind I have given you. It will serve you well. This is deep. You have truly never been here before. Many never come. It is OK. Embrace the uncertainty. Enjoy and take solace in the process. You know that things are happening. Draw peace and richness from the work I am doing in you. Discernment is the outflow of the wisdom that has come and has yet to come. Your spirit, heart and mind must work in concert with each other, as helpmates to one another. I have specific assignments for each. Each will help the others to bring to fruition the fullness of My plan in you. There is much more to know. Continue to yield to Me, My Child. I love you.

I understood the need to get out of my own way with great clarity. I realized that God was not the one holding me back, I was. I knew that He wanted me to continue my focus on Him while moving forward with this calling. I remembered an earlier leading Christ had given me to "meet Him there," which meant to step forward in faith with His guiding me in the process. He revealed that the plan would come into view as I continued to set my gaze on Him. I needed not be concerned at the present about the how things would happen. I only needed to be concerned about what He was asking me to do. In other words, take what I have gotten so far, and step out on faith. Do the work. Proceed with the speaking ministry. Move forward with the book. I had to make the time. There was an obedience that I had not stepped up to yet. And now, for the second time, God had laid on my heart to meet Him there. The longer I shrank back or refused to do it, the longer I would feel stagnant, and stuck in a funk. I realized I still had so much to learn, many ways to grow, and much more to experience. I also understood that a new chapter in my life had truly begun—or many chapters with God's blessing. I prayed that He would continue to guide me, to live through me and draw me closer to Him. I gave my Lord and Master, Jesus Christ, all the glory, praise and honor. He was everything. His patience was infinite. His grace was unending.

THE POINT

Jesus had truly become everything in my life. I counted the costs and I chose Him. I let everything else fall away until He was all that remained. I stilled my heart, opened my spirit and sought Him for who He is and for no other reason or reward. I accepted what He desired me to have. I was learning to discern reluctance and humility from disbelief and doubt. I realized that without Christ, I was unworthy, but in Him, He deemed me worth it. In Jesus I found rest and came to receive His love and comfort. I vowed to seek His face and walk with Him consistently, not occasionally or in a transactional manner but, in everything I did. I needed to know Him more, and learn to love Him better and more deeply. I had to allow Him to do the work I could not do and complete the work He had begun. I wanted God to show me the way to walk in purity and holiness with my anointing. I asked Him to direct me in using my gifts for His good pleasure and to teach me what I must know.

Through all of this, it became clear that Jesus was compelling me to move into a realm of intimacy that I had never experienced, and quite frankly, one that most Christians never experience. The more I accepted my mantle, the more I understood that this is now my charge. I am to draw closer to Christ and help others do the same. I am to wake Christians up, all Christians, to the reality that there is more. I am to wake up those that profess to be Christians but have not crossed the line of faith, and those who are believers but remain infants in the faith. Among these people, there needs to be great reparation of hearts. There needs to be a healing of wounds and a relinquishing of control that will allow God's children to bring their whole hearts to Him. Only hearts that have been reclaimed and restored by Christ can be given over fully to God.

And it is not only hearts that are in question, but minds, bodies and spirits as well. The requirement is to give every aspect of who we are over to God in obedience. This was what I had done and now continued to do day by day, more and more. Come to Him and remain. The point is to maintain intimacy with God. We are not to leave His presence. I desire to seek and request His presence continuously, while being a signpost for others on the journey.

We are to walk in His will and be obedient to Him and His desire for our lives. We should be feeling the presence of the Holy Spirit in everything we do, being counseled by Him every step of the way. We are to abide in the Lord's love, truth, grace and mercy in all things and at all times. Never leave. That is the example of Scripture. This is the relationship, the oneness with God that He has always intended.

That is my charge. I am to go forth so that those who have ears to hear can know beyond the shadow of a doubt that Jesus loves them deeply, that they matter to Him, and that He has more for them. He is the "More." Jesus Christ is the source. So now, the journey continues, when in reality, it has only just begun. I love You, God, Abba, Father. Jesus, I love You with all my heart, mind, soul and strength. Amen.

Bibliography

Davis, Mac. *In The Ghetto.* RCA Records, 1969.

Myers, Mike. *Wayne's World.* Paramount Pictures, 1992.

The Wachowski Brothers, *The Matrix.* Warner Brothers Pictures, 1999.

Eldredge, John. *Wild at Heart.* Nashville, Tennessee: Thomas Nelson Publishers, 2001.